# Critical and Applied Approaches in Sexuality, Gender and Identity

Series Editor
Christina Richards
Calver, Derbyshire, UK

This series brings together scholars from a range of disciplines who have produced work which both informs the academy and, crucially, has real-world applied implications for a variety of different professions, including psychologists; psychiatrists; psychotherapists; counsellors; medical doctors; nurses; social workers; researchers and lecturers; governmental policy advisors; non-governmental policy advisors; and peer support workers, among others. The series critically considers intersections between sexuality and gender; practice and identity; and theoretical and applied arenas – as well as questioning, where appropriate, the nature or reality of the boundaries between them. In short, it aims to build castles in the sky we can live in – after all the view is nothing, without a place to stand.

Shoshana Rosenberg • Damien W. Riggs
Salem Skelton

# The Trans Möbius Strip

## Gender Dysphoria Meets Gender Euphoria

palgrave
macmillan

Shoshana Rosenberg
Flinders University
Adelaide, SA, Australia

Damien W. Riggs
Flinders University
Adelaide, SA, Australia

Salem Skelton
Flinders University
Adelaide, SA, Australia

ISSN 2628-8141 ISSN 2628-815X (electronic)
Critical and Applied Approaches in Sexuality, Gender and Identity
ISBN 978-3-031-70785-8 ISBN 978-3-031-70786-5 (eBook)
https://doi.org/10.1007/978-3-031-70786-5



This Palgrave Macmillan imprint is published by the registered company Springer Nature Switzerland AG.
The registered company address is: Gewerbestrasse 11, 6330 Cham, Switzerland

# Preface

We recently read a paper in which the authors suggested that, to date, no one had yet to 'operationalize' the concept of gender euphoria. While the authors cite most of the papers we also cite in this book, their claim was that for gender euphoria to be truly understood and measured, it needs to be operationalized. For us, this constitutes a problematic turn in the field of trans studies. First, and as we explore in this book, building on the work of other trans scholars, trans peoples have long spoke about the concept of gender euphoria, which includes defining it in our own ways, while also recognizing that it cannot be defined: it is a shifting concept that has different meanings for each person. Second, and given the histories of 'operationalization' that have functioned to harm trans people (think of diagnostic manuals that operationalize our lives as 'disordered'), we must wonder how the operationalization of euphoria might be used to regulate, measure, and control trans peoples. And third, how might operationalizing gender euphoria co-opt into a transnormative agenda?

In this book we take something of a different path. While we certainly speak about both gender dysphoria and gender euphoria, including in terms of thinking through what each concept means, we also want to hold space. Hold space for the diversity of ways in which trans peoples understand these concepts. Hold space for resistance to both concepts. And hold space for how both concepts can be limiting. We hold space by introducing the figure of the trans Möbius strip, a figure, as we outline in Chap. 1, that functions precisely because it is never just one thing. Indeed, while in Chap. 1 we explore the figure of the trans Möbius strip, we never operationalize it. Instead, we situate it within a realm of possibilities, and in a relationship to other such concepts or figures that are not easy to pin down to one single thing or definition.

In working with the figure of the trans Möbius strip in this book, our intention is to engage in ongoing conversations within trans communities about how our lives are understood, lived, and shared. As three authors with very different experiences and backgrounds, we eschew the idea of a singular trans voice, instead writing at times as a collective, diverse, we, at other times one of us writing in the first person, and at other times writing about ourselves in the second person. Our intention in using these differing modes of writing is to ensure that the reader cannot easily deduce or impute a singular 'trans position' from our writing. Instead, the reader is encouraged to recognize that we sit as individuals within broader histories of trans writing that, collectively, constitutes a 'trans voice'. In other words, while individual trans people speak, there is no singular 'trans experience'. Instead, any idea of a 'trans experience' is collective, diverse, and multivocal.

The reader will also see, even from a simple glance at the contents page, that in this book we cover a diversity of overlapping topics, organized under general sections that themselves overlap. This overlapping, messy, at times repetitive way of framing the book is again intended to eschew any claim to a singular trans narrative, or a singular definitive account of either dysphoria or euphoria. Instead, in this book we work our way through many different ways of thinking about dysphoria and euphoria. Covering self-help, political activism, and rigorous academic thought, this book serves as but one entry point into an ongoing conversation about what it means to be trans. We hope our readers will continue on these conversations through and beyond our work.

Adelaide, SA, Australia — Shoshana Rosenberg
Adelaide, SA, Australia — Damien W. Riggs
Adelaide, SA, Australia — Salem Skelton

# Acknowledgements

We begin by acknowledging that we live on the unceded lands of the people of the Kulin Nations, the Peramangk people, and the Kaurna people. We acknowledge their sovereignty as First Nations people and affirm our commitment to working alongside them in their fight for autonomy and self-determination over their lives and traditional lands. We extend this solidarity to Palestine and Palestinians both in occupied territories and diaspora, and hope to see liberation for Indigenous peoples everywhere.

Our thanks must go to Beth Farrow, commissioning editor at Palgrave, for believing in this project from the very start. Our thanks also go to Clelia Petracca from Palgrave for taking up oversight for the book through the contracting process. Finally, thanks to Kishor Kannan Ramesh from Palgrave for support throughout the production process.

Shoshana would like to thank my dyke (and dyke ally) crew who have kept me present, focused, and full of righteous rage: Sophie Keeffe, choreboy, Nic Menser Hearn, Dr. Nida Mollison, Cher Tan, Lyla Shlon, Dan Thorpe, and Elsa Tuet-Rosenberg. Finally, thanks to Damien and Salem for collaborating with me and tolerating my allergy to haste and punctuality.

Damien would like to thank Shoshana and Salem for making this such an enjoyable project. Thanks to the young people with whom I have had so many conversations in the therapeutic space, all of whom informed this work. Thanks to all of the amazing scholars working in this space, whose work and lives inspired and informed me. Finally, thanks to the many clinicians I have trained, who have asked such thoughtful questions: I hope this book provides some of the answers.

Salem would like to thank Damien and Shoshana for believing in my abilities and valuing my contribution to this field. Thank you to my PhD participants whose thought-provoking interview responses sparked my interest in trans rage. Thanks to all my cis, trans, and non-binary friends for our illuminating discussions about gender which inspired and informed this work. A big thanks to my partner for listening to me while I fleshed out my ideas and for knowing how to support me with my dyslexia. Finally, thanks to my cat companion for keeping me company while I write.

# Contents

Part I Key Concepts 1

1 The Figure of the Trans Möbius Strip 3

2 Histories and Presents of Gender Dysphoria and Euphoria 13

3 Affirming Care Is Generalist Care 23

Part II The Body 31

4 Trauma in the Body and Affirming Care 33

5 Struggle in the 'Wrong Body': Crip and Trans Perspectives on Collective Euphoria 41

6 Fucking Euphorically, Fucking Dysphorically 55

Part III Euphoria-Forward Approaches 69

7 Relational Euphoria: Fractures and Healing 71

8 The Imagined Transpolitic and the Transsexual Intifada: Euphoria, Dysphoria, and Political Action 79

9 Clinical Interventions and Euphoria-Forward Approaches 91

Part IV Liberatory Euphorias 99

10 Euphoria Beyond the Binary 101

11 Euphoria and Spirit: G-d, Body Mod, the Transsexual Divine 115

12 Trans Rage for Everyone 129

Postface 141

Index 143

PART I

# Key Concepts

CHAPTER 1

# The Figure of the Trans Möbius Strip

## Introduction

In this book we mobilize the figure of the Möbius strip to think through what it means to be trans in contemporary global contexts. A Möbius strip is a three-dimensional strip twisted upon itself that upon first glance appears to have two distinct sides, but upon closer examination is actually a continuous loop with only one side. The figure of the Möbius strip is arguably most well-known through the work of Lacan, a French psychoanalyst. For Lacan, the single-sided figure that appears two-sided is helpful for understanding how concepts that might at first appear binary (e.g., love and hate, inside and outside) are in fact part of a continuum. That we cannot definitively state where on the continuum one ends and the other begins allows for the possibility of transversal: the crossing over between two states. While Lacan offers some of the possibly most well-known applications of the Möbius strip, in this book we opt to take differing starting places for our elaboration of a 'trans Möbius strip'. We are mindful that Lacanian psychoanalysis has been (and in some places continues to be) used as a weapon against trans people (though this is slowly changing, see Gherovici, 2017, and a special issue of the journal *TSQ*). While we cannot easily escape Lacan within theorizing about the Möbius strip, our aim in this book is to mark out new entry points for a trans Möbius strip,



S. Rosenberg et al., *The Trans Möbius Strip*, Critical and Applied Approaches in Sexuality, Gender and Identity,
https://doi.org/10.1007/978-3-031-70786-5_1

entry points that centre trans theorists as much as they rework existing (cis) feminist and psychoanalytic theorizing.

In this introductory chapter we outline some of the many levels at which a trans Möbius strip offers leverage for understanding contemporary trans experiences. Specifically, by introducing four distinct but intertwined levels we build a case for what it means to work with the image of a trans Möbius strip. In the remainder of this book we then apply this image across a diversity of contexts as they relate to both gender dysphoria and gender euphoria, as we outline briefly in the final section of this chapter, with the following chapter exploring both gender dysphoria and gender euphoria in detail. As authors living within, across, and through the figure of the trans Möbius strip, this work is both deeply personal while also being committed to contributing to spaces in which contemporary thought about trans people's lives can be grounded in concepts that are trans-centric. Taking a critical approach to trans people's lives as its starting place, then, allows us within this book to continue a dialogue with a long and rich history that is centrally shaped by a trans worldview.

## The Individual as a Node of the Social

Back in 1994, a collective of British critical psychologists, writing under the moniker of Beryl Curt, elaborated in detail the formation of the individual through the social. The moniker Beryl Curt was a play on the educational psychologist Cyril Burt, whose work on intelligence and heritability had long since been debunked. In their book *Textuality and Tectonics,* the authors who comprised Beryl Curt sought to explore what it means to think about 'individuality' in the context of discourse. As a gender and racially diverse group of people, Beryl Curt brought together a diversity of shared and unique histories to tease out how we might think about 'the individual' in primarily western contexts. The line of thinking outlined by the Curt collective was as much ground-breaking in these specific contexts as much as it was the introduction of centuries-old thought from other cultural contexts. Writing in 1997, for example, Oyêwùmí noted that the imposition of western gender categories onto the Yorùbá people (of Western Africa) ignores the fact that gender categories are not how Yorùbá people understand the world. As Oyêwùmí notes, relations between Yorùbá people are organized by sociality, rather than primarily being focused on the body (understood as a medicalized, individualized concept). Oyêwùmí explores how, while there are Yorùbá terms for differing bodies, these do not map across to western identities.

For Curt (1994), the individual is most appropriately understood not as a separate circle that sits within or upon a wider social circle, but rather as a loop of the social. If we think of the social—the institutions, ideologies, and discourses that circulate within a given culture—as a line, then each individual is a loop on that line. Much like the Möbius strip, the individual as a loop of the social emphasizes that there is no beginning nor end of 'the individual' as a stand-alone entity. Rather, 'the individual' is contiguous with the social. As Curt describes it, then, the individual is a 'node' of the social. How we come to understand 'ourselves' is a product of the institutions, ideology, and discourses made available to us, and through which we are constituted.

This understanding of 'the individual' is vital to understanding what it means to work with the figure of the trans Möbius strip. Discussions of, for example, trans peoples having 'internalized transphobia' very much miss the mark. All people living in societies that actively or implicitly promote forms of cisgenderism are interpolated by this ideology. To be a node in a sociality that is shaped by the assumption that assigned sex determines gender, and that there are only two genders (as but two forms of cisgenderism) is too formed through a relationship with these assumptions: our very being is shaped in response to the hail of cisgenderism, whether it be to try and approximate these assumptions (though never fully occupy them, as we discuss further below), or to refuse these assumptions.

Conceptualizing the individual as a node of the social, as we do in this book, takes up the challenge made by Stryker et al. (2008) to think about trans instead as trans-, with the inclusion of the hyphen intended to move beyond trans as a form of nominalization, and to instead think about trans- as a form of relationality. Relational in the sense that trans is formed through a relationship with cis (a point we explore further below), relational in terms of always existing in reference to cisgenderism as we noted above, and perhaps most importantly, relational in terms of trans communities and our ongoing negotiations and navigations of gender as a concept. As we explore further in the following section, trans peoples have always been at the vanguard of thinking through the sex and gender.

## Contiguity and Sex and Gender

While, as we briefly introduced above, concepts of sex and gender are not axiomatic across all cultures, in western contexts it is most certainly the case that sex and gender as concepts form a core part of the social of which the individual is a node. In saying this, we want to be clear that in speaking about the social we are not referring to some sort of external a priori bedrock that constitutes a factual basis through which the individual is formed. Rather, the social—again as a series of institutions, ideologies, and discourses—is formed through agreed upon norms, practices, and beliefs that are both static and in flux. This might seem like an odd claim to make: how is the individual—as practitioner of norms, practices, and beliefs—a node of the social that is formed through said norms, practices, and beliefs? Here we come back to the figure of the Möbius strip. As a node, the individual is both shaped by and a shaper of the social, just as the social is formative of and shaped by the individual.

When it comes to sex and gender, then, we all too often see sex framed as a bedrock based in the body, while gender is seen as a psychological overlay. By contrast, we follow cis feminist writers such as Grosz (1994) and Fausto-Sterling (2000) in viewing sex as a social construct that, yes, references bodies, but is framed through a particular cultural lens through which those bodies are made to matter (Butler, 2011). As Lacquer (1990) documents, understandings of sex have shifted across time, highlighting that while claims are made to the body, the body itself is constituted through discourse. This is not to deny the materiality of the body, but rather to suggest that the material is given meaning through discourse.

The idea that gender is an overlay to sex is itself a historically and culturally specific claim. In some accounts sex and gender are treated as one and the same thing (and specifically that sex determines gender). In other accounts, ones that are often framed as more progressive, sex is seen as the bedrock, and gender as an expression that signifies our affective relationship to our sex, such that sex does not necessarily determine gender. For us, by contrast, and following Grosz (1994) and Fausto-Sterling (2000), we view sex and gender as mutually constituted in the service of a particular social order. Situated on the same Möbius strip, it is impossible to say where discourses of sex end and discourses of gender begin. It is possible, however, to say that this strip is itself a discourse, one that is thoroughly social and through which the individual (in western contexts at least) is constituted.

It is increasingly the case that reference is made to 'affirming one's gender', in contrast to language that is now seen as dated, and which references 'changing one's sex'. Yet what does this substitution mean? We use the term 'substitution' here with intent. When gender is used instead of sex, and sex is left as the supposed material bedrock, how much has really changed when it comes to thinking differently about trans peoples' lives? Sex as the supposed bedrock is still weaponized as a tool against trans peoples. 'Gender diversity' becomes the province of trans peoples, with cis people still able to occupy a comfortable place within the norm of sex = gender.

The figure of the trans Möbius strip, as we will continue to unpack in this chapter, offers us a heuristic through which to view sex and gender differently. Through this figure, sex becomes something that is *done* to bodies, and which can indeed be 'changed'. If a woman has a sex that is female, then this is equally true for trans women and cis women, for example. What is changed here is one's relationship to discourses about sex and gender. If the Möbius strip of sex and gender means that the two cannot be easily discerned, then what changes is not some a prior 'fact' about sex or gender. Rather, what changes is our acceptance of a given set of rules about what constitutes sex or gender. If sex is gender as much as gender is sex, then who can claim a rightful place within any sexed or gendered category is up for grabs. While the current social fabric might not see this as the case, the figure of the trans Möbius strip would suggest otherwise, as we explore in more detail in the following section.

While the above might suggest that anything is up for grabs (and perhaps that is indeed the case), our suggestion is not to eschew that bodies are constituted in a diversity of ways. While the old two-sexed model has been surpassed by an understanding of a diversity of sex characteristics, this does not mean that sex as a category has been surpassed. By contrast, for us the figure of the trans Möbius strip suggests that there are bodies and their constituent parts, there are the cultural label attributed to those parts (i.e., some might be called a penis, some an arm, some a head, or some a clitoris), and there are also cultural meanings attributed to those same parts (everyone has a head, most people have two arms that function in relatively familiar ways—these descriptions are fairly generic, ableism aside—but it is *women* who have a clitoris, and *men* who have penis), yet these are all overlays. We can talk about bodies that gestate, and bodies that ambulate, and bodies that think, and bodies that produce sperm, without sexing those bodies, and certainly without gendering those bodies. And through the figure of the trans Möbius strip, we can think differently about what it means to change our relationship to commonly accepted cultural norms about what constitutes particular bodies.

## Trans and Cis as (Non-Oppositional) Modalities

When it comes to (primarily, though not exclusively, cis people's) accounts of trans people's lives, the language of 'identity' and 'identify' is replete. How often do we see 'so and so identifies as a woman', or 'so and so has a non-binary identity'? By contrast, this language is rarely applied to cis people. Cis women *are* women, for example. Importantly, however, Lowik (2022) introduces the language of 'identify as' in their work on trans people and reproductive healthcare to signify that no one actually occupies a particular gendered position by default. In other words, for example, no one *is* a woman, no one *is* a man. Rather, we are all approximations of these imagined categories that are shaped by discourse, rather than by particular bodies or psyches. Lowik introduces a praxis whereby *all* people 'identify with', not just trans people. In so doing, we are encouraged to remember, as per the section above, that sex and gender are not categories derived from an empirical reality, but are part of a discourse in which bodies (and identities) are made to matter.

While we enthusiastically share Lowik's (2022) position, we are also mindful of two things. First, the language of 'identifies with' or someone having a 'trans identity' continues to be wielded against trans people. While Lowik's project is one that seeks to resist and indeed reclaim this language for strategic purposes, we feel that this work must by necessity be done in strategic and perhaps piecemeal ways. To switch to 'identifies with' in a book that seeks to establish new ways of thinking about trans lives might be to jump the gun. In other words, it might well be the case that before we can reclaim 'identifies with' we need to continue to do the work of thinking through the situatedness of trans lives. Certainly, Lowik does this work, and is not in any way jumping the gun. But this book is a different project with its own starting place. Most definitely, in the trans Möbius strip there is space for both resisting and reclaiming 'identifying with', as we explore in this book.

Alongside Lowik's (2022) work, we are also mindful of Ansara's injunction to resist the cisgenderist assumption that trans and cis people constitute two entirely separate categories (Ansara & Hegarty, 2014). Indeed, this injunction sits neatly on a form of the trans Möbius strip with the work of Lowik. To suggest that all people 'identify with' a gender is similar to suggesting that trans and cis people are not categorically separate. Rather, as Ashley (2022) suggests, trans and cis are modalities that mark each person's relationship to cisgenderist norms about sex and gender, as we explored in the previous section. Overarching all three accounts, however, is what we see as claims to transness that also function as forms of resistance. While any conceptualizations of 'transness' could be read as a form of essentialism, in our reading they are instead claims to exceptionalism: that trans peoples hold particular insights about the operations of cisgenderism by dint of their forcible relationship to cisgenderism.

As such, our 'compromise' going forward in this book is to work with the rather unwieldy language of 'trans peoples'. The language of 'trans peoples' functions, we argue, to address Lowik's (2022) concerns about what it means to 'identify with' a gender. It addresses Ansara's concerns about not treating trans and cis as entirely separate categories (Ansara & Hegarty, 2014). And it takes on board Ashley's (2022) language about gender modality. The language of trans peoples constitutes a collective of people shaped by our relationship to cisgenderism, while not proposing a singular trans experience. The language of trans peoples emphasizes relationships, such that cis people are not treated as the opposing category. Rather, transness is viewed as a relational and flexible category while still having a 'core' constituted through discourse that is both formed in response to cisgenderism, while also constituting a novel relationship to said discourse that is not simply a damage-centred response. In the following section we take up in more detail what it means to resist damage-centred accounts of trans lives.

## The Dysphoria/Euphoria Nexus

When trans peoples' lives are spoken about, there is often a strong or sole emphasis on distress. This is a problem given that focusing on distress experienced by individual trans people ignores the broader ideological context in which trans people live, as we explored above. This is most evident when it comes to the often-concerted focus on 'gender dysphoria'. Reference to gender dysphoria as a way of describing trans peoples' lives often results in three individualizing and limited accounts. First, trans people are unilaterally viewed as being 'dysphoric', ignoring the diversity of experiences that trans peoples may have, including those for whom there is no dysphoria. Second, 'dysphoria' is treated not only as axiomatic but as unilateral. In other words, feeling dysphoria about one's body is treated as telling the entirety of the story about trans peoples' lives. Third, discussions about gender dysphoria often presume that the category 'dysphoria' holds common or even clear meaning. It is typical to find academic work on 'young people with gender dysphoria' that presumes 'dysphoria' as a known entity, or reduces it to a psychiatric diagnosis. Missing is a depth understanding of the lived experience of gender dysphoria.

These three individualizing accounts of gender dysphoria predominate in the literature and limit our understanding of the lived experiences of trans peoples, including in terms of limiting our understanding of what gender dysphoria means. Following Tuck (2009), we would describe this over emphasis on gender dysphoria as damage-centred. Damage-centred research, and more broadly damage-centred understandings of people's lives, emphasize only what is seen as harm caused or psychological distress experienced. Through this lens, trans peoples are too often seen as uniformly and unilaterally distressed by dysphoria, and that this causes harm. There are many things missing from this account. First, missing is a focus on the societal contexts in which gender dysphoria is produced, and specifically the context of cisgenderism, as we explore in more detail in the next chapter. Second, the over focus on gender dysphoria can at best ignore the agency of trans peoples, and at worst pathologize trans peoples. Damage-centred accounts of trans peoples' lives thus actually potentially do the opposite of what they intend: rather than primarily drawing attention to the needs of trans peoples, they may instead obfuscate them.

Yet as much as in this book we seek to move beyond damage-centred accounts, at the same time we do not wish to engage in forms of ableism that ignore the harms caused to trans peoples. As Baril (2015) argues, 'social accounts' of both disability and being trans too often deny the individual effects of marginalization. Social accounts are those that situate challenges associated with disability and being trans solely in institutions, ignoring the challenges that individual people might face regardless of how supportive (or not) institutions might be. As we will explore in the following chapter, cisgenderism constitutes a key context through which gender dysphoria is produced. But we do not wish to be over deterministic in making this statement. While cisgenderism is central to the production of experiences of dysphoria for many trans peoples, it is not the sole producer. It is important to recognize that for many trans peoples dysphoria is also existential. This might seem a circular argument: a person experiences dysphoria in an embodied and existential sense due to social norms that promote certain ideologies that bring dysphoria-as-phenomenon into being. Our argument in this book is that rather than seeing this as circular, it constitutes yet another turn of the trans Möbius strip. As a node of the cisgenderist social sphere, trans peoples are subjected to externalizing forces that produce dysphoria, but as per our arguments in the previous section, there are also exceptional aspects of transness that situate trans peoples within a unique relationship to embodiment.

In this chapter, then, we seek to focus on how gender dysphoria is framed at the societal level, before unpacking the differences between internal and external inputs or causes, leading us to question how the language of gender dysphoria has become so central not only to other people's understandings of trans peoples' lives, but also to trans peoples' accounts of our embodiment. In doing so we both challenge damage-centred accounts, while also recognizing the lived reality of gender dysphoria for many trans peoples. Accompanying our exploration of the meanings of gender dysphoria is a concerted (and indeed foundational) focus throughout this book on 'gender euphoria'. As we argue, gender euphoria is an important concept in its own right, offering as it does a way to understand trans peoples' experiences, at the same time as situating euphoria in a relationship to dysphoria. Again, as per the image of the trans Möbius strip, both are part of the same narrative, even if they function in potentially different ways.

## Concluding Thoughts

In this chapter we have introduced our conceptualization of the trans Möbius strip. In so doing we have hinted that we feel this conceptualization has broad application, not limited solely to trans peoples, a topic we take up further in Chap. 3. Rather than simply being an account of trans peoples' lives, then, the image of the trans Möbius strip is one that requires a fundamentally different account of sex, gender, and cisgenderism, as we have outlined in this chapter. The trans Möbius strip takes transness as a given, while also situating transness within a relationship to broader social forces through which and in opposition to it is constituted. In so doing, the trans Möbius strip provides us with theoretical and practical leverage through which to think about both gender dysphoria and gender euphoria that are not damage-centred, but which retain a focus on the regulatory functions of cisgenderism.

## References

Ansara, Y. G., & Hegarty, P. (2014). Methodologies of misgendering: Recommendations for reducing cisgenderism in psychological research. *Feminism & Psychology, 24*(2), 259–270.

Ashley, F. (2022). 'Trans' is my gender modality: A modest terminological proposal. In L. Erickson-Schroth (Ed.), *Trans bodies, trans selves: A resource for the transgender community* (pp. 22–26). Oxford University Press.

Baril, A. (2015). Transness as debility: Rethinking intersections between trans and disabled embodiments. *Feminist Review, 111*(1), 59–74.

Butler, J. (2011). *Bodies that matter: On the discursive limits of sex.* Taylor & Francis.

Curt, B. C. (1994). *Textuality and tectonics: Troubling social and psychological science.* Open University Press.

Fausto-Sterling, A. (2000). *Sexing the body: Gender politics and the construction of sexuality.* Basic Books.

Gherovici, P. (2017). *Transgender psychoanalysis: A Lacanian perspective on sexual difference.* Taylor & Francis.

Grosz, E. (1994). *Volatile bodies: Toward a corporeal feminism.* Indiana University Press.

Lacquer, T. (1990). *Making sex.* Harvard University Press.

Lowik, A. J. (2022). "I gender normed as much as I could": Exploring nonbinary people's identity disclosure and concealment strategies in reproductive health care spaces. *Women's Reproductive Health, 10*, 1–19.

Oyêwùmí, O. (1997). *The invention of women: Making an African sense of western gender discourse.* University of Minnesota Press.

Stryker, S., Currah, P., & Moore, L. J. (2008). Introduction: Trans-, trans, or transgender? *Women's Studies Quarterly, 36*, 11–22.

Tuck, E. (2009). Suspending damage: A letter to communities. *Harvard Educational Review, 79*(3), 409–428.

CHAPTER 2

# Histories and Presents of Gender Dysphoria and Euphoria

## Introduction

In the first chapter of this book we introduced the concept of the trans Möbius strip, suggesting that in multiple ways this figure allows us to think differently about trans peoples' lives specifically, but all people's lives more generally in terms of living in a relationship to cisgenderism. In that chapter we also introduced both gender dysphoria and gender euphoria as concepts that, while often seen as separate, operate within the trans Möbius strip. While in Chap. 3 we will explore how this applies to all people, in this chapter we focus specifically on how both concepts function in the lives of trans peoples. This might seem like a back to front approach: going from the specific in this chapter to the general in the next chapter. We do this purposively for a number of reasons. First, while we see the figure of the trans Möbius strip having applicability to all people, we are centrally concerned with its operations in trans peoples' lives. Second, it is to trans peoples that categories such as gender dysphoria and euphoria are most commonly applied. Looking at how these categories are applied to or derived from trans peoples' lives is thus an important starting place. And third, like any good application of the figure of the trans Möbius strip, there is no 'obvious starting place'. The general might be the starting place in a typology where we derive the specific experience from the



S. Rosenberg et al., *The Trans Möbius Strip*, Critical and Applied Approaches in Sexuality, Gender and Identity,
https://doi.org/10.1007/978-3-031-70786-5_2

general. But in our account of the trans Möbius strip, this does not have to be the case. Rather, in reading this chapter and Chap. 3 together, we will argue that the general and the specific are deeply enmeshed, with no easy beginning or end.

Importantly, this chapter is not intended to be a detailed account of either gender dysphoria or euphoria. While accounts of the latter are only starting to emerge in academic and popular writing, accounts of dysphoria are seemingly endless. With this in mind, we map out a potted history of gender dysphoria first, mindful that dysphoria is not necessarily the thing that comes first. In other words, while the documented history of dysphoria as a concept might be longer, this does not mean that euphoria has not been around for as long as trans people have existed (i.e., forever). In mapping out a potted history of dysphoria, our aim is to signal the twists and turns through which gender dysphoria has become so codified as a concept, and how that differs from, and potentially adds limits to, how people experience dysphoria as a psychological and embodied experience. Following this we explore growing conversations about gender euphoria, with an explicit focus on countering any idea that euphoria is the conceptual 'opposite' of dysphoria, or indeed that euphoria should be treated as the ideal 'affirming' outcome for all trans peoples. In our potted history of gender euphoria, we are also focused on the disaggregation of euphoria as a concept that is differentially experienced, rather than again positing a singular understanding.

## Histories and Presents of Gender Dysphoria

In 1974, Norman Fisk published a paper titled 'Gender Dysphoria Syndrome', which as far as we can identify, constitutes the first academic evocation of the concept of gender dysphoria. In the paper Fisk defines gender, conflating psychological and physical concepts under the one banner, and uses a dictionary definition of dysphoria as a referent for dissatisfaction. Inherent to his definition is the idea that trans peoples experience dissatisfaction with our gender, which is reliant upon the cisgenderist definition of gender as identical to sex. Leaving aside these issues of lexicon, across the paper Fisk outlines why the conceptualization of gender dysphoria became important to him and his clinical colleagues. As he notes, prior to this conceptualization his clinical team had only accepted for medical treatment people who conformed to a very narrow image of the 'true transsexual'. This required people to report long-standing (i.e., since childhood) feelings of being a particular gender, and that not being able to live as that gender resulted in extreme levels of distress. Fisk noted that increasingly he and his colleagues saw standardized narratives being presented, which in some cases they felt was not actually an accurate description of 'true transsexualism', but rather was a narrative created in order to access medical care. In response, rather than excluding people they suspected were not 'truly transsexual', Fisk and his colleagues broadened their eligibility category through the lens of gender dysphoria. This meant that, within reason, and still according to their decisions as the clinicians, people who had only more recently come to understand their gender, or who did not experience high levels of distress, might be eligible for treatment.

Of course, nothing is ever as easy as simply endorsing more people to access the care they needed. Certainly, Fisk's own account is highly pathologizing, but can nonetheless be construed as at least somewhat affirming. By contrast, Fisk shares the problems raised by colleagues who were entirely opposed to any form of care for trans people. As Meyerowitz (2004) notes, in countries such as the United States 'mayhem laws' were often evoked to claim that removing a body part as part of affirming care constituted a breach of both the sovereign individual, and the sovereign nation state. Surgeries that would 'damage' otherwise 'healthy' bodies was viewed as an attack on the ableist and cisgenderist idea of the 'natural born body', as well as constituting a broader threat on the military industrial complex that required bodies to be 'complete' in certain ways so that they could be enlisted for war. Returning to Fisk, he notes that some of his colleagues viewed affirming surgical care for trans people as immoral and 'tantamount to medical malpractice' (p. 390).

Such concerns, in the face of clinicians who sought to provide affirming care to a broader number of people, ultimately resulted in the codification of gender dysphoria in ways that meant the breadth of potential recognition was in some ways reduced. In other words, rather than being a catch-call form of categorization that eschewed stricter requirements associated with the 'true transsexual', gender dysphoria, and particularly under the *Diagnostic and Statistical Manual* of the American Psychiatric Association, has since again become a way to sift out who might be deserving of medical treatment, and who might not be. While organizations such as the World Professional Association for Transgender Health in its *Standards of Care* does not require a formal diagnosis of gender dysphoria, it is certainly the case that many clinicians require such a diagnosis, a requirement that at least in part constitutes a reason for why the diagnosis remains in the *Diagnostic and Statistical Manual*. While a secondary argument is that its inclusion provides ways for people to claim against their health insurance, either way the inclusion of a formalized diagnosis of gender dysphoria serves to engender gatekeeping.

In many ways, then, we are back to the concerns that Fisk was trying to avoid, namely, the scripting of clinically acceptable narratives of being trans that are treated as required in order to access affirming care. This type of scripting can be either done purposively to circumvent gatekeeping, and/or it might be done through a desire to conform to transnormative understandings of trans lives. Transnormativity refers to homogenized or normative accounts of what it means to be trans (Riggs et al., 2019). This can include the presumption that all trans peoples want access to medical treatment, to all be viewed as cisgender (hence eschewing a trans-specific aesthetic or mode of embodiment), and that all trans peoples affirm the language of being 'born in the wrong body'. It is indeed this latter language of being 'born in the wrong body' that holds particular sway when it comes to accounts of gender dysphoria (Namaste, 1996). Certainly, for many trans peoples, inhabiting a body that does not reflect our understanding of our gender is distressing. This is an existential matter, reflecting that gender is a deeply felt affective dimension of being, one that is also reflected in our embodiment.

Yet dysphoria is also produced at the institutional or ideological level when media reports, for example, repeatedly reiterate the language of 'born in the wrong body', providing trans peoples and our loved ones without a positive way to think about trans lives. Indeed, as Roen (2019) suggests, not only is dysphoria (and its presumed corollary of distress and self-harm) treated as axiomatic, but it is too often treated as the sole route to intelligibility for trans peoples. What this means is that in order for trans peoples to be happy, or to at least experience happiness through our embodiment, they must counter not only any dysphoria they may experience, but also counter *other people's* expectations about what it means to be trans. In other words, what does it mean for the trans person who does not experience dysphoria? Or what does it mean for the trans person who is okay with their trans embodiment (i.e., they do not strive for a semblance of being cisgender, or indeed if they are proud of their trans body as it is)? Such people may be rendered less than or unintelligible within dominant narratives about trans young people and embodiment. There is very much the sense, then, in which trans peoples are damned if they do, and damned if they don't, when it comes to being in a relationship with the dominant dysphoria-centred account of trans embodiment. If trans peoples emphasize experiences of dysphoria, including potential self-harm, then our experiences may be treated as intelligible, but these are experiences that centre upon distress and leave little space for joy. Conversely, if trans peoples resist dominant dysphoria-centred accounts, they may be viewed by others as 'not really trans', or as 'not trans enough' (Ashley, 2019).

As we can see, then, gender dysphoria is so often treated as a taken for granted, indeed expected, fact in trans peoples' lives, so much so that rather than functioning to offer a more inclusive approach as was the intention of Fisk and his colleagues, it instead functions to regulate and control. Indeed, so axiomatic is the category of 'gender dysphoria' that we increasingly see academic papers using the language of 'gender dysphoric children' or 'children with gender dysphoria', language that treats this descriptor as having inherent meaning, or as usefully telling us something about how said children understand themselves and their lives. Our point is not to dismiss here that some trans peoples experience dysphoria, we noted this above, but instead to continue the work of examining how, within the trans Möbius strip, (often clinical) accounts of dysphoria serve to both reify it, and treat it as axiomatic. In the next section we shift our focus to gender euphoria, though again mindful that due to cisgenderism the two function alongside one another.

## Histories and Presents of Gender Euphoria

We were very thankful that ahead of us writing this chapter, Jacobsen and Devor (2022) published an empirical paper on gender euphoria, in which they provide an overview of the history of this concept. As they note, the term has been used within trans communities for decades, first being documented not long after Fisk documented use of the term gender dysphoria, as we explored above. In 1976, Ariadne Kane compared euphoria as comfort in living with dualities to 'true transsexuals' who solely felt dysphoria (cited in Jacobsen and Devor, 2022). As Jacobson and Devor also note, ten years later the term gender euphoria was used in the title of a newsletter published by the Boulton and Park Society (cited in Jacobsen and Devor, 2022). As such, while empirical research on gender euphoria remains relatively thin, as Jacobson and Devor outline, the concept itself has existed formally for almost as long as had the concept of gender euphoria, not to mention that trans peoples have most certainly experienced joy throughout time.

In terms of how we understand the concept of gender euphoria, authors who have taken a more desire, joy, and pleasure-based approach to researching trans lives have tended to focus on the wide variety of emotional descriptors and diverse experiences associated with positive gender-related feelings. Such descriptors of gender euphoric feelings include: acceptance, achievement, affirmation, alignment, authenticity, comfort, congruence, ease, joy, relief, satisfaction, and validation. These feelings can arise in response to medical and social transition processes, being recognized and affirmed as one's gender by others, alignment between internal sense of self and embodied reality, mastery of gender performance as a skill, community engagement and solidarity, positive media representation, hopeful imagined futures, and through the self-talk that arises as a result of these beliefs and positive experiences (Skelton et al., 2023). The fact that there are so many emotional descriptors and examples of experiences applied to feeling gender euphoria speaks to its complex and multidimensional nature. As such it can be a difficult concept to succinctly describe. Regardless of how it arises or is described, however, euphoria's positive impact on trans people's well-being and engagement with the wider world is evident in research which show improvements in quality of life, increased self-esteem and body positivity, and the development of meaningful connections with others as a result of experiencing euphoria (Davis, 2022; Shuster & Westbrook, 2022).

Importantly, however, we are mindful of the assumption that gender euphoria is an antidote to gender dysphoria, both metaphorically and literally in the case of taking hormones. This can lead to some trans peoples having potentially unrealistic expectations of how gender-affirming care will make them feel and may subsequently experience disappointment when the outcome they are hoping for proves elusive. Gender euphoria often centres around ideas about 'passing', and this creates an environment in which the goal of gender-affirming care becomes less about how one feels inside and more about how one is seen and treated by others. The gender euphoria comes once people see and treat you differently than they were before, but if they're not treating you differently or if they're treating you worse, then complicated feelings can arise that may lead to blaming yourself for your perceived inability to fit into yet another cisgenderist category. Much like the body positivity and 'self-love' movements, or at least what these movements have become, gender euphoria sets a standard that is not realistically achievable for all trans peoples, nor is it necessary for our health, happiness, and potential to thrive. If we are to strive for what is effectively seen as the second-best option; self-acceptance or acceptance of how we are perceived by others, are we also giving in to a cisgenderist notion of what it means to experience gender and thus allowing this notion to continue to go unchallenged? What does gender euphoria even mean in a cisgenderist society anyway? Does it mean replicating the oppressive norms already laid out but just from the 'other side' and if so, where does this leave non-binary people? What does gender euphoria mean to an agender person, for that matter? If gender euphoria is held up as the ultimate goal for trans peoples, then does this concept invalidate agender people's existence out of hand? These are questions that we will return to in Chap. 10.

It is important, then, not to place gender euphoria on a pedestal, as this runs the risk of falling into the toxic positivity and commodification of happiness trap that has pervaded, and sometimes co-opted, social justice spaces (Shuster & Westbrook, 2022). In doing so euphoria can become part of a transnormative narrative in which trans people are expected to adhere to a mode of temporality based on desiring a normative future where they can only feel good about, and in, our bodies once they have received gender-affirming care and are read by others as cisgender. Transnormative narratives depict transition as a linear path from pre-transition, in which one is disembodied in one's assigned gender, through mid-transition and an unmooring of the self, to post-transition, characterized by embodiment of one's gender and thus feeling euphoria. A nuanced understanding of euphoria requires that we view it not as an end goal nor as an overriding of dysphoria, but as a form of resilience that can assist trans peoples in coping with potential dysphoric distress and forge their own understanding of what it means to be trans, outside of transnormative expectations (Jacobsen & Devor, 2022).

Trans experiences are complex, and they are both composed by and transcend normative temporalities. While the autobiographical narrative of transformation and self-actualization may be a mode of temporality which encourages conformity to normative frameworks, it also has significance for those trans peoples who do find empowerment, comfort, and healing in being able to track their transition progress. At the same time, when these narratives are restricted to transnormative guidelines they still inevitably reinforce the pathologization of transness. Amin (2014) speaks to the merit of considering trans experiences through a lens of trans temporality that runs counter to the rigidity of the transnormative narratives that autobiographical transition stories often abide by. Trans temporality is a term used in reference to the 'social patterning of experiences and understandings of time' (Amin, 2014, p. 219). It is one in which the legitimacy of a trans person's gender is not determined by medical transition. In resisting time-restricted, linear, transnormative transition narratives, trans people create unique alternative temporalities which blur the lines of past/present/future. In pursuing knowledge about gender euphoria as it exists in the temporalities of trans lived experiences, we can disrupt the current damage-centred style of knowledge production, challenge the notion that trans bodies are inherently sites of discomfort, distress, and suffering, propose alternative temporalities for trans timelines, and promote the resilience that already exists within trans peoples and trans communities.

## Concluding Thoughts

In this chapter we have briefly mapped out some of the histories of gender dysphoria and gender euphoria, hinging our arguments on key turning points where each concept has formally come into being, and from there exploring some of the twists and turns leading to how each is now most commonly understood. For dysphoria this has involved a journey from dysphoria potentially being an expansive (if still gatekeeping) concept, to one that is now relatively limited in terms of who meets the diagnostic criteria (though we would note that within the *Diagnostic and Statistical Manual* it is possible to provide a diagnosis of 'other specific gender dysphoria' or 'unspecified gender dysphoria' for people who do not meet the diagnostic criteria, though these are themselves still diagnoses that emphasize distress). Gender euphoria, by relative contrast, has since its inception focused on joy for trans peoples, though as we have explored in this chapter, there is always the risk that euphoria becomes a mandate regulated by transnormative ideals.

Our discussions in this chapter, then, highlight not simply that dysphoria and euphoria often occupy the same trans Möbius strip in terms of sitting within broader cisgenderist narratives (even if in resistance to them), but further that they do not necessarily tell all of the story of transness for all trans peoples, a claim that we explore in many of the chapters that follow. In the next chapter, however, we take up some of our explorations of gender dysphoria and euphoria when we consider the suggestion that gender affirming care is in fact universal care applicable to all people.

## References


Amin, K. (2014). Temporality. *Transgender Studies Quarterly, 1*(1–2), 219–222.

Ashley, F. (2019). Thinking an ethics of gender exploration: Against delaying transition for transgender and gender creative youth. *Clinical Child Psychology and Psychiatry, 24*(2), 223–236.

Boulton and Park Society. (1987). *Gender euphoria, 1*. Retrieved from https://www.digitaltransgenderarchive.net/col/1v53jw986

Davis, A. (2022). *Trans joy: Celebrating diverse transgender narratives*. Unpublished Honours thesis. The University of Tennessee.

Fisk, N. M. (1974). Gender dysphoria syndrome: The conceptualization that liberalizes indications for total gender reorientation and implies a broadly based multi-dimensional rehabilitative regimen. *Western Journal of Medicine, 120*(5), 386–391.

Jacobsen, K., & Devor, A. (2022). Moving from gender dysphoria to gender euphoria: Trans experiences of positive gender-related emotions. *Bulletin of Applied Transgender Studies, 1*(1–2), 119–143.

Kane, A. (1976). Historical and cultural perspectives on crossdressing. The Provincetown Symposium. Retrieved from https://www.digitaltransgenderarchive.net/files/g732d898n

Meyerowitz, J. (2004). *How sex changed: A history of transsexuality in the United States*. Harvard University Press.

Namaste, K. (1996). Theory's erasure of transgender subjectivity. In B. Beemyn & M. Eliason (Eds.), *Queer studies: A lesbian, gay, bisexual, and transgender anthology* (pp. 183–203). New York University Press.

Riggs, D. W., Pearce, R., Pfeffer, C., Hines, S., White, F., & Ruspini, E. (2019). Transnormativity in the psy disciplines: Constructing pathology in the *Diagnostic and Statistical Manual of Mental Disorders* and *Standards of Care*. *American Psychologist, 74*, 912–924.

Roen, K. (2019). Rethinking queer failure: Trans youth embodiments of distress. *Sexualities, 22*(1–2), 48–64.

Shuster, S. M., & Westbrook, L. (2022). Reducing the joy deficit in sociology: A study of transgender joy. *Social Problems, 71*, 1–9. https://doi.org/10.1093/socpro/spac034

Skelton, S., Riggs, D. W., Pullen Sansfaçon, A., Katz-Wise, S. L., Arora, M., & Thibeault, C.-A. (2023). It just feels realty nice when people call me by my name': Accounts of gender euphoria among Australian trans young people and their parents. *Journal of Gender Studies, 33*, 470. Online First.

CHAPTER 3

# Affirming Care Is Generalist Care

## Introduction

In 1949 French philosopher Simone de Beauvoir published *The Second Sex,* in which she argued that one is not born but rather one becomes a woman. By this de Beauvoir meant that while a person may be assigned female at birth, this does not make them a woman (or a girl). Rather, it is through processes of stereotyped socialization that some people are, in effect, trained to enact the social position of 'woman'. This argument is, to a large extent, in line with the language we introduced in Chap. 1 from Lowik (2022), namely, that people 'identify as' a particular gender. Even more recently, Lavery (2023) has again reiterated that early feminist work (and in particular white feminist political organizing) centrally argued that 'woman' was a category marked by political disenfranchisement, not by biological unity. When it comes to women, then, no person actually occupies the place of 'the woman'. Rather, all people who are assigned female and who experience themselves as girls and then women engage with and repeat the culturally available norms available to them. Certainly, all people in the category 'woman' do this in a diversity of ways: again, there is no 'one woman'. de Beauvoir argued, as is evident in the title of her book, that women are always viewed as secondary to men (within a binary logic), a hallmark of women's subjectivity.



S. Rosenberg et al., *The Trans Möbius Strip*, Critical and Applied Approaches in Sexuality, Gender and Identity,
https://doi.org/10.1007/978-3-031-70786-5_3

We begin this chapter with a brief discussion of de Beauvoir to reiterate our figure of the Trans Möbius strip, this time in the form of a question about what constitutes gender affirming care. Too often, 'gender affirming care' is language reserved solely for trans peoples. Trans peoples are seen as needing access to medical and psychological treatment that will 'affirm' our gender. Yet what might it mean to think about all medical care, and many aspects of psychological care, as gender affirming for all people. Our argument in this chapter is that rather than thinking about care for trans peoples as exceptional (which often means limited specialist services, long wait times, and legislative gatekeeping or indeed outlawing of care for trans people), it is important to think about how all people access care that in one way or another supports their experience of their gender, and how this sits in the broader context of what Paul B. Preciado (2013) terms the pharmacopornographic era.

Also important to include in this chapter is an exploration of what it means to live in places where gender affirming care is not available, where it is becomingly increasingly regulated or restricted, or if it is available, it is more available to some than others. The second half of this chapter thus briefly explores restrictions on access to care, and how trans peoples specifically resist incursions upon our rights to access care, and what this means for experiences of gender euphoria. In part our argument in this chapter is that, viewed through the lens of the Trans Möbius strip, all care is by default gender affirming in one way or another. Yet at the same time, whether or not care is accessible appears to rest upon the fault lines of gender modality, hence in places in practice turning the Trans Möbius strip into a binary of haves and have nots. In the face of this, trans peoples claim and reclaim ways of engendering access to care within community, even if at the same time as we might want to recognize that more broadly many aspects of gender affirming care for all people are regulatory and reliant upon cisgenderist and sexist accounts of what it means to inhabit a particular body.

## All Care Is Gender Affirming

In his book *Testojunkie*, Preciado (2013) argues that practices of pharmacology rest upon histories of animal testing, eugenics, commercialization, and the inculcation of humans into capitalist logics of commodification. This is equally true for both trans and cis peoples. Moreover, current practices of hormone administration are deeply embedded in histories of trans medicine, with the identification of hormones as something understood to be playing a key role in the regulation of all bodies in the context of western medicine, and the first requests for affirming medical care for trans peoples, occurring largely alongside one another. Yet when we think about 'affirming care', all too often this rests upon the presumption that our referent is trans peoples.

Yet as Schall and Moses (2023) argue, beyond hormone therapies, histories of affirming care are again histories of care that have largely been directed towards cis people, even if they have also at times been utilized by and for trans people. Think about the development of genital surgeries to people affected by wars, or reconstructive surgery for cis women following mastectomy following cancer treatment. Or think about the development of testicular implants for cis men following cancer treatment, or the development of puberty blockers for (nominally) cis children experiencing precious puberty. These are all examples of gender affirming care that equally apply to trans and cis lives, yet for cis people they are typically just referred to as 'surgeries' or 'care', with 'gender affirming' left out of the picture.

Following Schall and Moses (2023), we would suggest that so many of the treatments all humans receive are gender affirming. If, as a cis man, our understanding of our body includes having testes, then any surgery (such as in regard to cancer) that requires their removal, affects our sense of our gender. Testicular implants, then, are gender affirming surgery. The same is true for cis women who undergo reconstructive surgery following breast removal. Certainly, not all cis people do these things or make these choices. For some, the removal of particular bodies of their body reflects nothing about their gender, so no further surgeries are undertaken. But it is fair to say that for many cis people further surgeries are often at least considered.

The same is also true for medication. Think of cis men taking medication to prevent or treat baldness, or cis men taking Viagra. These are both practices that speak to cis men's feelings about their gender, as Preciado (2013) has argued so deftly. Yet so often these practices are just treated as men doing what men have to do, not as something people categorized as men do to maintain their place within that category. All of these practices as undertaken by cis people, many of which are also undertaken by trans people, are all forms of gender affirming care, but again, so often for cis people such treatments and practices are covered by insurance or public health as they are seen as (gendered) matters of necessity, whereas for trans people they are not.

So why do we see this point of differentiation? Central to this differentiation is arguably the cis/trans binary, in which cis people are treated as the norm. Medical procedures that cis people undertake are treated as standard, but when trans peoples undertake them it is seen as exceptional. This is largely a product of cisgenderism: cis people are seen as just doing things that enhance their existing bodies, or indeed keep their bodies in the state they were 'intended' to be. Trans peoples, by contrast, are seen as going against what our bodies are 'intended' to be, and hence medical treatment is seen as exception (think back to the mayhem laws we wrote about in Chap. 1).

In many ways this exceptionalism is what makes 'gender affirming care' seen as such a 'positive step', when it is simply the provision of necessary generalist care. Despite this, trans people repeatedly report that when they seek to access such care—care that would typically be provided to cis people with little hesitation—medical professionals balk. They claim not to have 'specialist knowledge', or claim that trans medicine is beyond the scope of their practice (Gieles et al., 2023). Certainly, there are some surgeries that may be seen as trans specific (e.g., phalloplasty, vaginoplasty), yet in reality they are not. Phalloplasties have long been performed for cis men wounded in war. Vaginoplasty has long been performed on intersex people—often through coercion—to manufacture idealized vaginas (i.e., to accommodate penetrative heterosex).

Treating care for trans people as exceptional 'gender affirming care' thus allows for gatekeeping, it allows it to seem as though trans people are receiving some kind of 'special care' not afforded to others, and it serves to position medical care for trans people as contentious. This is a topic we take up in the following section.

## Restrictions on Access to Care, and Euphoric Resistances

In some legislatures, access to care for trans people is restricted, either on the basis of age, or insurance, or location, or any number of factors that may prevent people from accessing care. In other legislatures, access to care for trans people is entirely banned and indeed is illegal. In some legislature where care is currently available, moves are being made to restrict or ban access. None of this is new. Texts documenting trans histories clearly and repeatedly speak to attempts to stop trans people from accessing care. From the refusal to treat children (Gill-Peterson, 2018) to highly restrictive access for adults (Meyerowitz, 2004), trans peoples' access to medical care has always been tightly regulated.

Yet throughout time, trans peoples have crafted ways to affirm our gender through bodily modifications. Taylor (1996) conjectures that Enarees, nomadic Scythians living in the fifth century, found ways to create womanly bodies through the consumption of horse urine (from which Primarine was originally synthesized) and through horse riding (causing scrotal abnormalities). While we must be careful about imposing the category 'trans' onto these peoples, and while the Enarees did not leave a written record of their practices, we can nonetheless see that changing one's body has a long history.

Playdon (2021) does an amazing job of documenting how men such as Ewan Forbes, in the context of the United Kingdom, found ways to navigate affirming care in the early 1900s. While his journey was fraught, and most certainly made possible due to his social status, he was not alone in navigating care in the face of legal prohibitions. What marks out cases such as those of Forbes is the secrecy required, secrecy wrought by the effects of cisgenderism, but which nonetheless leave a legacy in terms of transphobic accusations on the part of cis people directed towards trans peoples. Should it be any surprise that trans people have often, and still, feel the need not to disclose that they are trans, for fear of retaliation or refusal or service? Think too of Agnes, the young girl who convinced medical professionals that she was intersex, having all along taken her mother's hormone medication (see the wonderful documentary by Joynt & Schilt, 2022). While Agnes is often framed as deceptive, instead we see her as someone who made an agentic decision in a particular political and historical context in order to access medical care.

Somewhat more recently, there are the wonderful stories of Eilís Ní Fhlannagáin and her collaborators, who provided surgeries to trans women in the early 2000s from a barn, using materials bought on eBay (Dodds, 2022). Growing from fear and suspicion on medical doctors, in combination with issues associated with medical insurance and reticence on the part of professionals to provide medical care to trans women, Ní Fhlannagáin provided care to many trans women: care that was life-saving in many ways. The telling of stories such as these are often euphoric in nature, highlighting resistance to institutionalized practices, and the capacity of trans women to provide for themselves.

Similarly, in the wake of calls for and the implementation of bans on healthcare for trans peoples in some parts of the United States, trans people have developed ways of sharing medications. Twitter has been awash with people offering to connect one another with prescriptions from interstate, or to post medications. This echoes long histories of so-called 'black market' access to medications and other treatments for trans people. While it is absolutely the case that such access has often been highly problematic if not fatal (such as quacks allegedly injecting silicone for trans women, that in reality was tyre filler), it nonetheless highlights community organizing in the face of refusal of access to care, as evidenced in recent research on the topic of DIY hormones (August-Rae et al., 2024).

So often in research stories about medical tourism, the stories of trans people travelling or moving in order to access care are left out of the frame (though see Aizura, 2018). And again, research on, for example, cis people travelling to Asia to undertake commercial surrogacy, or for cheap cosmetic surgeries in Eastern Europe, is not typically viewed as gender affirming. But when trans people—by necessity—travel to access care, or engage in practices that help to secure access to treatments not available in their area, it is treated not simply as gender affirming, but as illegal, questionable, and problematic.

In this section we have but touched on the long histories of trans peoples accessing medical care, or creating access to such care. These are but a small handful of a much wider narrative of trans people who have found ways, in the face of prohibitions, to gain access. Too often women such as Lili Elbe are trotted out to speak to the long histories of trans peoples accessing care, when in reality these histories span much longer periods of time, and provide examples of trans people acting on their own, helping one another, navigating difficult systems, and doing so often outside the realms of authorized medical care. That this has been, and continues to be, necessary highlights the ongoing effects of seeing care for cis people as non-gendered and essential, and care for trans people as specialist and restricted.

## Concluding Thoughts

As has been true in the previous chapters in this book, this chapter provides a brief glimpse into the worlds that trans peoples navigate, and has suggested that viewing care for trans people as only that which constitutes 'gender affirming care' ignores that so much of medical care is in fact gender affirming. Seeing care for trans peoples as exceptional sets us up as peoples to be regulated, and indeed to be denied access, or only to receive access on very specific, narrow terms.

If, instead, we return to the figure of the trans Möbius strip, we can see that many of the histories we briefly outline in this chapter demonstrate the intertwining of 'trans medicine' and many other fields of medicine, with cis people often benefiting from 'trans medicine', just as trans people ourselves have been at the vanguard of creating pathways and the need for certain forms of care. There is no generalist and specialist care. Rather, there is what Preciado (2013) terms the pharmacopornographic nature of all medical care that inculcates us all into particular gendered regimes of embodiment.

## References


Aizura, A. Z. (2018). *Mobile subjects: Transnational imaginaries of gender reassignment.* Duke University Press.

August-Rae, B. C., Baker, J. T., & Buzzanell, P. M. (2024). 'Not just rebellious, it's revolutionary': Do-it-yourself hormone replacement therapy as liberatory harm reduction. *Social Science and Medicine, 345*, 116681.

de Beauvoir, S. (1949). *The second sex.* Librairie Gallimard.

Dodds, I. (2022). 'Never ask permission': How two trans women ran a legendary underground surgical clinic in a rural tractor barn. *Independent,* July 3.

Gieles, N. C., Zinsmeister, M., Pulles, S., Harleman, A., van Heesewijk, J., & Muntinga, M. (2023). 'The medical world is very good at cis people, but trans is a specialisation'. Experiences of transgender and non-binary people with accessing primary sexual and reproductive healthcare services in The Netherlands. *Global Public Health, 18*(1), 2246059.

Gill-Peterson, J. (2018). *Histories of the transgender child.* University of Minnesota Press.

Joynt, C., & Schilt, K. (DIR). (2022). Framing Agnes.

Lavery, G. (2023). Gender criticism versus gender abolition: On three recent books about gender. *Lost Angeles Review of Books,* July 31st.

Lowik, A. J. (2022). "I gender normed as much as I could": Exploring nonbinary people's identity disclosure and concealment strategies in reproductive health care spaces. *Women's Reproductive Health*, 1–19.

Meyerowitz, J. (2004). *How sex changed: A history of transsexuality in the United States.* Harvard University Press.

Playdon, Z. (2021). *The hidden case of Ewan Forbes: The transgender trial that threatened to upend the British establishment.* Bloomsbury.

Preciado, P. B. (2013). *Testojunkie: Sex, drugs, and biopolitics in the pharamapornographic era.* Feminist Press.

Schall, T. E., & Moses, J. D. (2023). Gender-affirming care for cisgender people. *Hastings Center Report, 53*(3), 15–24.

Taylor, T. (1996). *The prehistory of sex: Four million years of human sexual culture.* Bantam Books.

# PART II

# The Body

CHAPTER 4

# Trauma in the Body and Affirming Care

## Introduction

Having established, in the first section of the book the key concepts we are working with, in this second section we continue with our explorations of the trans Möbius strip by focusing closely on the body and trans peoples. Certainly, as we argued in Chap. 3, the arguments we present in this book should not be read as limited in application solely to trans peoples. Many of the topics we explore throughout this book are equally applicable to cis people. Yet as we have also stated repeatedly, there is something unique and specific about the experiences of trans peoples that warrants concerted attention. In this chapter our concerted attention rests with experiences of trauma, and how these play out within the context of affirming care.

It is nothing new, of course, to state that many trans people experience trauma. Trauma wrought by living in a context of cisgenderism. Trauma wrought by intentional and unintentional violence caused by other people. And trauma wrought simply by being a human living in this time. Indeed, trauma, while not always named as such, is a core focus of much of the research in the field of trans studies, perpetuating as it does unintentionally a damage-centred approach. Clearly a focus on trans peoples and trauma is necessary, given so many trans people experience trauma. Yet there is also a sense in which the documentation of trauma or its simplistic



S. Rosenberg et al., *The Trans Möbius Strip*, Critical and Applied Approaches in Sexuality, Gender and Identity,
https://doi.org/10.1007/978-3-031-70786-5_4

theorization potentially does very little other than to state the obvious. Needed, then, are other ways of thinking about trauma and trans peoples.

The trans Möbius strip offers us a lens through which to think about trauma in different ways. Firstly in this chapter, we think through what it means to work with trauma in the lives of trans peoples. While Chap. 9 specifically focuses on euphoria-forward approaches to clinical work, in this chapter we set some of the groundwork for that chapter by using our conceptualization of the trans Möbius strip to consider what it means to listen and respond to embodied experiences of dysphoria, with a focus on how these play out specifically for people who may newly be discovering their transness. As a counterpoint, however, in this chapter we then explore how affirming care itself can be another site of trauma. While accounts of care provision to trans people are replete with examples of discrimination and gatekeeping, we want to push such accounts further by considering how they may be sites of trauma.

Obviously, the claims we make in this chapter are not intended to discount the utility of affirming care. Yet at the same time, in the rush to insist upon affirming care in the face of ongoing attacks directed towards both trans peoples and those who provide affirming care (including trans clinicians themselves), it is important that we consider how any application of affirming care in the present sits in a relationship to histories (and presents) of clinical interventions that have not simply been damage-centred, but which have actively caused harm to trans peoples. In a sense, then, this chapter speaks both to trauma and to ethics: what does it mean to work ethically with trans peoples when trauma is so omnipresent.

## Trauma, Loss, and Embodiment

Some of the initial thoughts for this section came via Damien's engagement with the work of Belinda Chaplin, and particularly her PhD work (Chaplin et al., 2018). In this work, Chaplin explores the experiences of trans people who had undertaken gender affirming surgery, focusing on embodied experiences of change post-surgery, including in terms of feelings of loss. As a trans woman, Chaplin's work provided key insights into topics that are often sidelined, in favour of a narrative of joy, if not euphoria. Make no mistake: Chaplin's participants were all happy with the outcomes of their surgery. This is not a narrative of regret. Yet still, many spoke about being ill-prepared for inhabiting a body that was so changed, even if that body was a desired body.

In our rush to affirm the importance of gender affirming surgery, we run the risk of marginalizing aspects of affirming care that may not always be so positive. Certainly, there are reasons for why this might be the case. Given the constant attacks against trans peoples and the provision of affirming care, any narratives that speak of loss, or trans people who are not 100% happy following surgery, run the risk of simply providing material for those who wish to claim that gender affirming surgery should not occur at all. Yet when our accounts of affirming care are driven by a desire to present a happy narrative, what kind of disservice does this do to trans peoples?

First and foremost, then, our task is to find ways to talk about affirming care in ways that recognize dualities. The trans Möbius strip provides us leverage to do just this. As Damien so often emphasizes to the young people he works with, receipt of medical care (whether that be medication or surgery or both) has to sit in the context of a life that is experienced as worth living. This is most certainly a tall order: to support trans peoples to see life as worth living when for some, especially when waiting to access or receive medical care, can make life not seem living at all. The problem, however, is when receipt of medical care is presumed to be a cure all. Certainly, medication or surgery can make one feel as though one's body is how it should be. There is no doubt about that. But feeling that your embodiment is correct and feeling that *you* are correct are not necessarily one and the same thing.

Further, there is sense that for many trans people there is a marked turning *away* from the body as a means to cope with distress. This turning away from the body can mean that for some trans peoples, a body that eventually comes to be one that they are happy (or at least willing) to live in can be experienced as something of a stranger. There is a sense of this in the work of Chaplin, where many of her participants were seemingly ill-prepared for what it would mean to inhabit their reconfigured body. This does not mean they regretted change. Rather, they were just not prepared for it.

Damien has had many opportunities to speak with trans young people who, having disclosed their transness, are then awaiting some form of medical response. This holding period is painful for many people, and indeed a time of intense vulnerability for many trans peoples. Yet, as Damien explored with one young person in particular, this period of slow change is also painful for other reasons besides the wait. For this young person, the joy of living as themselves and being supported by their family was offset by loss. This loss, we discovered through careful conversation, was not the obvious and often talked about 'loss of privilege'. Certainly, there are losses in a cisgenderist world to not being cisgender. Loss of relative safety, loss of the taken for granted, and for some people, loss of loved ones. But there are other existential losses too.

For this young person, recognition of being a young woman was both an endpoint and an interminable starting point. To acknowledge and state that one is trans is a momentous turning point, but it also opens the door to so much. For this young woman, it involved asking who am I as this woman, what does she want, who will she be, and how does she let go of things that she viewed as part of her former assumed gender. As we unpacked these feelings, we came to see that some of the loss was about a compulsion to let go of her past, as though it couldn't reasonably be part of her present and future. The work involved laying aside the shackles of gender norms, where certain behaviours are treated as markers of a particular gender. This was a journey she had not expected, instead presuming that stating her transness would solely be freeing, as well as also opening the door to new challenges.

To embody one's gender, then, as a trans person, can take us to many places, places that often cannot be predicted. Certainly, being affirmed in one's gender, and having access to medical treatment (should this be desired), is essential. But essential also can be difficult conversations about what it will mean to inhabit a desired body, what might be experienced as a loss and why, and recognition that inhabiting one's desired body is not a cure-all, even if it can be an important part of being happy to inhabit one's body.

## Trauma in/and Affirming Care

The term 'affirming care', when used as an umbrella term for any trans-affirming medical care, can have a flattening effect on the realities of many of these interventions. Part of the processes of trans assimilation and the formation of transnormativity (which we will discuss further in later chapters) relies on the minimization and suppression of the more visceral aspects of trans life, including the reality of what a medical transition entails. Regardless of how these interventions are packaged, affirming care often necessitates certain traumas in order to exist at all. The bodily traumas of a scalpel cutting flesh, debilitating and painful recovery processes, and the eventual psychophysiological shock of inhabiting a reconfigured body are all embedded within the transition process.

This reconfiguration, our reintroduction to a body that feels and looks and functions in a radically different way, carries with it a traumatic potential. We have to reconnect with microscopic aspects of ourselves and relearn their functions, sensations, and even meanings. Chests now unburdened by excess tissue move differently under clothing, highlighting an absence as much as signalling the arrival of a more affirmed body. Genitals transformed by this or that intervention must be wrestled with and thoroughly recomprehended, as the sites of pleasure and function have been radically altered. Words like 'chest', 'cunt', and 'cock' need to be revisited or (re)reimagined, which requires attending to the histories of those embodied sites and the fresh reminders of our biological modifications. This is a painful process, and one which needs to be treated with the attention and care any radical transformation would require.

The most significant thing one might notice when looking in the mirror after such interventions is neither euphoria nor dysphoria, but simply a stark *difference*. The process of contending with this differentiation, of bridging the embodied and emotional gap between a past self-image and a post-alteration self-image, carries with it a certain ontological trauma (Bass, 2000). It is a disturbance to a core aspect of our understanding of ourselves, and its reintegration cannot occur without psychological processes of recovery. To look away from this reality in favour of creating a sanitized, simplistic, and family-friendly image of gender affirming care is to refuse to engage with some of the most potentially transformative aspects of medical gender transition. Trauma in this sense does not necessarily carry a negative connotation, but it does imply an irrevocable shift between who a person was before and after such a profound metamorphosis (Malabou, 2012). In attending to these sites of potential psychological trauma, we are better equipped to contend with the unavoidable ramifications of these psychophysiological alterations.

It also vital to consider the psychological traumas of undergoing medical transition in the context of contemporary transgender healthcare. While Real-Life Experience and other oppressive models of trans healthcare have largely disappeared, trans affirming care still occurs within a transphobic and heteronormative world. There is an immediate trauma at the access point to these interventions, as we are forced to contend with cisgender clinical gatekeepers and their inherently skewed perspectives on trans people. Whether they are well-meaning but unknowledgeable, cutthroat and business-oriented, or actively disinterested in the well-being of trans peoples despite their own clinical specialization, the majority of trans clinicians are unlikely to provide trans care that is truly connected with trans peoples' experiences and by extension their unique needs. Sometimes the consequences for this disconnect are minor or even imperceptible, but at other times the impact of the disconnect between trans affirming care 'experts' and their chosen specialized population can produce long-lasting emotional and physical trauma.

Affirming medical interventions occur within the most intimate spaces and circumstances. From the vulnerable position as a patient seeking a gatekept treatment from an over-empowered clinician, across the many physical examinations and blood tests and other arenas where the body is poked and prodded, all the way through to the surgical theatre where a naked, unconscious trans person places their entire existence in the hands of another person. These situations are highly charged and can be traumatic on their very own, without any relational specificities. Any person who has undergone a genital examination as part of their trans healthcare assessment[1] will attest that no matter how sterile and context-free these types of experiences are presented to be, they are invasive by their very nature.

This is not to conflate invasiveness, discomfort, pain, or even physical scarring[2] with either trauma or dysphoria, but to highlight the inherent tension of the innermost aspects of affirming care. This tension can be diffused by a truly attentive clinician, an inclusive clinical environment, and other ways of minimizing the impacts of this forced vulnerability. But the tension can also erupt (either intentionally or unintentionally), revealing the traumatic potential of these circumstances. Whether it's a slip of the scalpel or a slip of the tongue, when the margin of error is overstepped in such intense situations, there is a potential for permanent harm and subsequent trauma.

However, the way this potential manifests, and the grip it holds on us, is not entirely out of our control. We cannot control the fact that the majority of trans surgeons and specialists are cisgender, and that many of them inevitably harbour transphobic views and are therefore more likely to

[1] Whether due to clinical necessity or simply the callous procedure of an outdated clinician.
[2] Which many transsexuals wear with pride.

violate these vulnerable spaces through their careless words or actions.[3] We cannot control what happens when we are under the knife, or how our bodies will react to these surgical modifications. But we can control our self-perception, and our position in relation to any physical and psychological trauma/interventions we may undergo. We can harness the discipline which has brought us out of the closet, out of the ligatures of a cisnormative world, and use that same discipline to carefully attend to ourselves as we are reintroduced to our altered bodies. We can use these transformative opportunities to defy binaries such as pleasure and pain, euphoria and dysphoria, 'pre' and 'post-op'. If we reimagine affirming care not as a set of static milestones but as a part of a broader ongoing generative experience, we can see how the traumatic aspects of those experiences can too be recontextualized.

This section is not designed to frighten readers away from undergoing medical transition, and certainly does not align with TERF claims around the 'irreversible damage' caused by these treatments and surgeries. Rather, we want this discussion to inform your perspective on how affirming care is mispresented by both good and bad faith actors. On one side are those trans advocates and pro-trans clinicians who do not include the complexities of dysphoria and body image in their considerations and discussions, which can undermine the very real concerns of people at the start of (and across) their medical transition journey. On the other side are TERFs and trans-exclusive clinicians and health professionals of all stripes who present all medical transitioning as an agonizing, unnecessary, and/or ineffective solution to a sociocultural problem.[4]

Both parties would like you to turn away from the truth of medical transitioning. Medical transitioning is a radical act of body modification that exists at the bleeding edge of current surgical and medical knowledge. It is an enormous (meta)physical undertaking, and must be approached with the highest regard. Medical transitioning, surgery in particular, is taking your own physical existence and remoulding it to fit your deepest desires. Therefore, there is as much potential for joy, pleasure, and euphoria as there is for disappointment, anguish, and dysphoria. Medical transitioning demands attention, care, introspection, self-forgiveness, self-love,

[3] Shoshana: I am reminded of a friend who, despite her protests, was referred to as a man throughout her entire hospital stay while undergoing vaginoplasty with one of the more internationally renowned trans surgeons.

[4] See Pearce et al.'s 'TERF Wars' (2020) for more on these narratives.

courage, and perhaps most importantly *time*.[5] If we provide those things to ourselves as well as we can throughout these experiences, we are sure to see blooms amongst the weeds, if not entire fields of wildflowers. Such is the case with any radical self-transformation: its yield is only as good as how well its demands are met.

## Concluding Thoughts

As we've explored across this chapter, the interactions between affirming care and trauma are far from simplistic. In order to better understand how our own (altered) embodiment affects our sense of grief, loss, and hurt, we need to understand the underlying narratives of transitioning, euphoria, and dysphoria. It is also vital to hold the contradictions of affirming care, and in particular surgery, in our minds: that something as radical as medical transitioning can yield both immeasurable joy and self-fulfilment as well as disappointment, pain, and trauma. Our attention, care, and attunement to ourselves and others within these intimate and vulnerable experiences can transform that pain and disappointment, and we have the tools to create experiences of embodied redefinition that are transcendent and euphoric.

## References

Bass, A. (2000). *Difference and disavowal: The trauma of Eros*. Stanford University Press.

Chaplin, B., Cox, L., & Campbell, C. (2018). Researching marginalized populations: Methodological challenges in transgender research. In *SAGE research methods: Cases* (pp. 1–18). Sage.

Malabou, C. (2012). *The ontology of the accident: An essay on destructive plasticity*. Wiley.

Pearce, R., Erikainen, S., & Vincent, B. (2020). TERF wars: An introduction. *The Sociological Review, 68*(4), 677–698. https://doi.org/10.1177/0038026120934713

[5] Of course it also demands significant money and resources.

CHAPTER 5

# Struggle in the 'Wrong Body': Crip and Trans Perspectives on Collective Euphoria

## Introduction

Disability is a sticky thing. We mean that in all the ways you can define 'sticky': it oozes, clings, leaves a residue that is often indelible. When our collective imagination conjures up an image of disability it inevitably veers towards the same polarities: those too mad or intellectually disabled to be conversed with, and those too crippled or housebound to be seen by the world. Each polarity its own tragedy, a thick curtain of misfiring neurons and self-betraying physiologies separating cripples from the rest of the world. Sickness has been positioned as ontologically separate to the rest of humanity, an innate point of division that cannot be alleviated.

In Susan Sontag's (2013) taxonomy of illness, disability in the contemporary world is ultimately understood entirely through the lens of cancer: a withering, unstoppable force that is materialized from within. The mythos of disability, of crippledom, acknowledges that violence sows seeds of physical and psychological dysfunction while ignoring what causes those seeds to bloom. It has become a cliché to say: 'you have to deal with your stress or you'll grow a tumour', an admonishment that isolates the cause of pain and suffering within an individual body. Our bodies and their health and well-being have become atomized, placing the responsibility of survival and care, as well as the blame for any failures to 'adequately' care



S. Rosenberg et al., *The Trans Möbius Strip*, Critical and Applied Approaches in Sexuality, Gender and Identity,
https://doi.org/10.1007/978-3-031-70786-5_5

for oneself, squarely with each individual (Greaney & Flaherty, 2020). It is nigh on impossible to contend with sickness or madness without falling further into the depths of those conditions (Taylor & Gold, 2019). The distance between the ill and their communities, between what needs to be done and access to the tools necessary for the task, is ever-growing.

Shoshana: *I'm writing my portions of this chapter from my home, where I have spent the vast majority of my time over the past several months due to my body giving in, at long last, after sustaining itself through a difficult year. Yes, it's true, I did not rest and now my body has taken it upon itself to force me inside, into bed. It's also true that you do not want to experience what I experience: pain so intense I often wake up and go to sleep nauseated, alarmed at the seemingly endless flow of aches and spasms that come from the historical violences that my bodymind re-enacts daily. These same experiences of pain can be applied to my experience of gender and transsexuality, a convoy of bodily sensations and mental images that at their worst feel like a straight edge blade slipping across my throat, if not a captive bolt to my temple. Blunt or sharp, fleeting or clockwork or constant, these are my daily companions. In my personal life, I have become a pull-cord toy, with catchy phrases such as 'rest now before your body does it for you' and 'slow down or you'll end up like me' coming out whenever that little internal mechanism is activated. It is as tedious and boring as it is a failure on my part to tell the whole truth: that perhaps ending up like me is not such a bad thing.*

By now you are hopefully beginning to understand that this is not a book about transgender suffering. Similarly, this chapter is not about trans cripple suffering. Instead, we want to explore the light side of shadowy subjects, to recover hope from the debris of lives that have been pathologized, essentialized, and tragedized to the point where they border on cartoonish. This process is an extension of the resistance to what Eve Sedgwick (2003) defined as paranoid reading, the deeply embedded 'emergency brake' sensation many of us feel when we even so much as contemplate touching complexity with anything but a surgeon's or archivist's gloves. There is an implied danger in discussing transing your sex or becoming disabled as anything other than a source of micromorts; what if, in discussing the beauty of these seemingly wretched experiences, we disavow the personal and collective suffering that existing in these ways brings about? Are we risking our status as marginalized peoples by looking beyond our oppression and towards the ways in which our lives can be liberatory, radical, and deeply meaningful? In a world that already seeks to discount our emotions and gaslight us about our very real experiences of abuse and ostracization, it can feel both politically and emotionally jarring to say that many of us *love* what these experiences have given us. But that is the truth, and the nexus of these experiences provides incredible insight into the euphoria of 'wrong bodies'.

## When Is a Body Wrong?

As long as there has been empire and colonization there have been 'wrong bodies', bodies which throw wrenches in the gear of linear colonial narratives of health, relationships, and bodymind experiences and expectations. Bodies which defy gendered expectations have been directly labelled as 'wrong' within Western medical contexts since the 1800s (Dominic, 2021), with surgical and medicinal interventions being viewed as a means of 'righting a wrong' (Sullivan, 2008). Disabled peoples' bodies have been similarly positioned as wrong, as they exist in direct opposition to the core tenets of Western colonial life (Clapton & Fitzgerald, 1997). Bodies which exist outside of Western colonial functionality—'broken' bodies, bodies requiring additional care, bodies whose narratives cannot be easily harnessed to the ideals of colonial life—are viewed not only as dissident but also in many ways as ***disem-bodies***, as abnormalities which exceed or fall short of the taxonomical definition of humanity (Grech & Soldatic, 2015). A 'wrong body' is one which is incapable of being harnessed towards capitalist perceptions of humanity, and is therefore of no economic (and by extension societal) value (Irving et al., 2017).

The question 'when is a body wrong' therefore needs to be answered on multiple fronts. When is a body wrong? When it bucks against notions of capitalist productivity and colonialist efficacy. When is a body wrong? When a body finds itself in the strange company of the fabled 'healthy, normal' people who supposedly make up the majority of society. When is a body wrong? When it asks for more than it can give. When is a body wrong? When it lies down when it is supposed to stand, or when it refuses to lie down when it is commanded to. When is a body wrong? Right now, always, or never, depending on your perspective.

It is also important that we do not fall into the trap of isolating bodies from minds. While 'wrong bodies' are often identified through visual difference, minds/brains[1] which function 'wrong' are inevitably found out through social interactions. The mad, hyperactive, autistic, narcissistic, or otherwise 'neurodivergent' (Legault et al., 2021) have become their own subclass of 'wrong' bodies, with their so-called 'divergence' demarcating a sharp turn away from the dominant neurotypical milieu and towards society's outskirts. For the rest of this chapter, we will deviate from this division and use the term 'wrong bodyminds' to further explore this phenomenon.

Clearly, our use of the word 'wrong' has remained in quotation marks throughout this chapter for a reason. Fundamentally, the notion of a bodymind that is unequivocally 'wrong', incorrect, malformed, or otherwise expendable is a core aspect of eugenics (Carson, 2016), and by extension fascism. We hope it is clear that our use of this language carries a sneer as well as an adamant disavowal. More importantly, analysing the notion of a 'wrong bodymind' allows us to further comprehend the cold and calculated mindset which underpins these ideologies. Not only are those of us considered 'wrong' consistently moved to the sidelines of society, but we become statistical errors, nameless and faceless anomalies which need to be removed in order to refine the formula of a perfect society.

Considering this destruction and erasure of 'wrong bodyminds' across colonial history, it can be easy to view the personal and collective life-worlds of cripples, trans people, and others considered 'wrong' to be entirely subject to the violence of those with 'correct' bodyminds. In fact, that is a core goal of these ideologies: to imbue the mere idea of such an existence with so much stigma, fear, and disgust that any person who finds themselves in these categories will either become isolated from society or self-annihilate in a misguided attempt to 'repair' these 'wrongs'. But if this supposedly perfect project was so effective, this book would never exist. If violence and suppression was all it took to extinguish particular modes of embodiment and existence, if these lives were truly so miserable so as to induce total ostracization or reparative suicide, we would have never heard of them—but we have. That means that no matter what, there are always those of us with bodies, minds, personalities, and attitudes deemed wrong by the broader world who are running free and spreading word of our existence.

[1] Used here interchangeably.

## Who Will Free Us?

There is a trend in both crip and trans studies to reach back towards earlier moments in history for examples of 'wrong bodymind' triumphs over 'normal' society. We have pedestaled particular moments in time—Stonewall, crip die-ins, the AIDS crisis, Mad Pride—as leading examples of our revolutionary roots. Those moments, at least in the grand mythology of the Revolution, paved the path for liberation of 'wrong' bodyminds. However, history has its limit, and tends to drag at the tip of the coattails of contemporary reality. We therefore need to zoom back into this century, this decade, this year, to truly discuss matters of the body.

In the present moment, in the year 2024, as this book is being written, both transness and disability have found themselves merged into a broader struggle which has been stirring just beneath the surface of global politics for decades—Palestinian liberation and the global Intifada. The Zionist entity's escalation of violence in Gaza in October 2023, combined with unprecedented levels of documentation through social media, has brought the issue of 'Israel's occupation of Palestine to light in unprecedented ways. At the time of writing, more than 30,000 Palestinians have been murdered by the 'Israeli' Occupying Forces in Gaza, along with casualties in the West Bank, Lebanon, and Syria. These are not new atrocities, as 'Israeli' settlers have always used extreme and armed violence to maintain control over Palestinians and their land (Gazit, 2015). What is new, however, is the global mobilization in solidarity that has transpired over the past few months.

While trans and crip solidarity with Palestine is not new, the scale of collective and collaborative solidarity efforts seems to have reached new heights. Palestinians' struggle against their oppressors, particularly in response to Israel's post Al-Aqsa Flood Operation escalation, has highlighted the ways Zionism (and its colonialist and imperialist birthing parents) destroys what it deems as 'wrong bodyminds' with impunity. Claims of Palestinian homo/transphobia, 'animalistic' social structures, or any other anti-Arab and Islamophobic tropes ring hollow when faced with the heartless and indiscriminate annihilation of Gazans at the hands of the 'Israeli' regime regardless of their gender, sexuality, or dis/ability. Witnessing such totalizing violence with such a singular focus has led many crips and trans peoples around the world to the same conclusion: our struggles *must* be intertwined, or else we are all betraying ourselves and our kin.

The call from Palestinians is not to take pity, patronize, or rescue them as if they are a helpless people. The call is to see our own experiences reflected within theirs, and join their resistance against oppressive forces. We are not asked to bring queer or trans rights to Palestine, but to see the existing struggle of those communities under Zionist occupation (Alqaisiya, 2018). We are not asked to take a critical crip theory lens on the subject of Palestine, but to see how Palestinian resistance is already an active disability justice movement (Wong, 2023). As is often said, Palestinians will free themselves, the question is whether we will be standing beside them when they do. We are being invited to free ourselves and each other in this process of solidarity.

## Schrodinger's Revolution

'Freedom' is perhaps too loose a term, particularly when considering long-term liberation struggles such as the Palestinian resistance. Freedom is contextual, fluid, and most assuredly not something that can be measured in rigid milestones. We did not mention Palestine in this chapter as another example to be historicized and set in stone(wall). Rather, the global Palestinian freedom movement (otherwise known as the global Intifada) shows us what happens when we refuse the binary of perpetual oppression versus an intangible and unimaginable utopia. The former guarantees the perpetuation of unnecessary suffering and death, while the latter paralyses us with its endless idealisms and intellectualization. The solution must be found elsewhere. There is a point between staring at the ground in submission and staring into the featureless sunny horizon until our corneas corrode. That point is the political moment we find ourselves in.

This returns us to the notion of the trans Möbius strip, and the effect of illusory multifacets in place of a singular reality. What we are witnessing when we consider the active, material reality of revolution is the dissolvement of both despair and idealistic rumination. There is plenty to despair about, yes, and we must hold in our hearts a vision of the world that is better than it currently is. But when treated as a binary, both polarities can lead to inertia, disconnection, and in more extreme circumstances either one's destruction or the destruction of another. If our choices are either to accept doom and perpetual war or view any less doomed futures as entirely utopic, then we remain bound by our own mind. Both positions consider the past as monolithic, the present reality as immutable, and the future as inevitable—all of which ultimately disempowers us and leaves us entirely subject to external forces.

Fortunately, this binary of struggle and dreaming collapses into a single experience when considered in the context of collective, revelatory, transformative actions. The Palestinian struggle for liberation, as well as the continuing actions of radical cripple and transsexual groups, are profound examples of how material[2] resistance forces idealism and despair together until they inevitably merge. In this state, despair under oppression becomes a motivating force, and we begin to bridge the gaps between our present reality and those brighter futures through the use of that force. Rather than disarming one another (by creating a depression vs. delusion binary), these forces become alchemical, intermixing to create new revolutionary realities. Much like Schrodinger's Cat, the only way to reveal the true nature of our future, and the worth of our past struggles, is by opening the box ourselves. Otherwise, we are left wondering.

## Locus of Euphoria

With these considerations in mind, we can see the same machinations at play in the realm of dysphoria and euphoria. Dysphoria in many ways functions as a type of 'reparative self-annihilation' mentioned previously; it is an ingestion of 'wrong bodymind' ideology which positions the ingester as the ultimate cause of their suffering. One of the fundamental issues of contending with dysphoria is the complexity of factors which ultimately create it. Dysphoria is too often simplified down to individual emotions and self-understandings, a sense of inner 'wrongness' that urges trans people to 'take action' against it. But it is precisely the matter of taking action, of having inner feelings which motivate externalized movement, which draws our intention to some of the ways dysphoria is manufactured from without.

In the same way that we will never live in a world without sickness or disability, we will also never live in a world without gender discomfort. Bodyminds shift and change, accidents (both happy and unhappy) are bound to occur, and the reality of human nature above all else is constant destruction and reconstruction. Both disability and transness are therefore inevitably affected, and co-created, by the world. Everything that grows inside us, both blooms and weeds, is at least partially seeded from the

[2] And armed.

outside. For this reason we must look at both dysphoria and euphoria through a critical lens, rather than relegating these emotions entirely to the realm of our inner worlds.

Trans euphoria, like dysphoria, remains connected to certain personal milestones within the public imaginary—euphoria from medical affirmation, 'passing', and gender-affirming actions, that is, becoming involved with more activities which one sees as aligned with their gender experience. But if we are the sole arbiters of our gender, why would there be dissatisfaction and anguish? If our dis/pleasure with our gender was entirely a matter of our personal actions, it would get done away with rather quickly. If dysphoria is understood as a fundamental sense of misalignment, then surely euphoria is its panacea! While this perspective can be comforting, and even a protective factor, it obscures the price of entry to this type of euphoria.

It is impossible to discuss any individual euphoria-oriented interventions without considering not only the financial cost but other hidden implications. When we focus on individual practices of affirmation, and centre discussions of euphoria on what one person can achieve in their personal life, we inevitably leave out those who cannot access euphoria through such channels. How can our actions be considered revolutionary when they uphold individual over collective growth? How can we experience personal euphoria while others are suffering? This is not to say that gender-affirming medical care is bourgeoise or selfish, but rather that we are only given options for fulfilment which come with significant compromises. Transnormative notions of where our *locus of euphoria* sits place both the burden and the pride of self-actualization entirely within our inner world and our individual influence. This position forces us to drown ourselves in our personal narratives and to prioritize our personal goals over those of our collective. Similarly, if all crip euphoria amounts to is wheelchairs and a lack of medical debt, then we have truly set the bar too low and left our poor, isolated, and marginalized kin in the dust of personal triumph. We are once again upholding individual experiences euphoria, or their absence, as our guide points.

This is why we must investigate where else the *locus of euphoria* could be placed, and what the impact of this movement might be. Specifically, we must look at the effect of placing our *locus of euphoria* neither entirely within us or completely outside of us. The former is often fleeting, costly, and ephemeral, while the latter leaves our fate entirely in the hands of the society we live within, which is unlikely to fulfil our needs. This results in dysphoria filling the vacuum euphoria has left, like running from one brief spot of sunshine to another through torrential rain. What is lacking is continuity of the kind that could never be sustained by any one person. This can only be facilitated by placing the *locus of euphoria*, for ourselves and others, within kinship.

## Euphoric Kinship Amongst 'Wrong Bodyminds'

Our use of the term 'kinship' here is aligned with Haraway's (2016) explication on the concept, which extends kinship beyond detectable lines of identity (or even species) and towards a continuous, conscious, political process of kin-making. These are the processes already taking place amongst those who have eschewed the siloing of identity politics in favour of harnessing themselves to the process of creating coalitions against oppression. In fact, kinship is the only way many of the world's most marginalized peoples continue to exist. Kinship makes up for what capitalist, fascistic, white supremacist nations actively take away. It is only through kinship that many of us access care (Gzesh, 2022; Kafer, 2019), express ourselves (Halberstam, 2016; Quinn, 2023), and work collectively towards opposing these systems which want us dead and forgotten. Kinship is not intellectual, but meta/physical labour that asks of us to see the risks associated with any radical move towards freedom[3] (Lake & Dagostino, 2013) and to strive towards them anyway. This is not self-annihilation, but a reclamation of power in the process of annihilation we are already deep within. It is through our relationships, our shared stories, and our collective action that we resist the ultimate goal of fascism: our complete destruction.

Political kinship is a lifelong process, rather than a static vision of an ideal future. It is also a move against the traditional use of kinship as a means of maintaining power within small, interconnected families or other groups (Thelen & Alber, 2017). This process asks us to challenge our desires and alignments, witness both the longevity and unpredictability of our potential lifespan, and consider how we can harness ourselves to movements and communities which extend back generations and will exist well past our personal expiration dates. These tasks are not assigned to us by a higher power or institution, but rather they are the most glaringly necessary responses to the material reality of our world. Political kinship

[3] Including those most extreme risks, i.e., severe injury or death.

prioritizes collective well-being, and sees the ways individuals invariably benefit from this collective focus (Morris, 2018). These are the fundamental principles of creating mutually beneficial microworlds of resistance with ever-expanding boundaries, and merging our struggles with others who are oppressed.

If kinship is the political framework, euphoric kinship is one lens through which we can understand the embodied effects of that framework in action. Before we go any further, it is important to note that while the term 'euphoric kinship' could imply the existence of dysphoric kinships, the proceeding paragraphs will show that any notion of 'dysphoric kinships' are ultimately an oxymoron. We are using the term 'euphoric kinship' to shine a light on processes already in place, on emotional and spiritual and political landscapes which are thriving and can be accessed by anyone who takes on this work. Euphoric kinship is the outcome of kinship work, if it is allowed to be.

It is undeniable that the processes discussed so far have an urgent political motivation behind them, first and foremost. But political urgency can be meagre, unpredictable fuel, especially in the context of decades-long struggle. We therefore have to look at what other psychological states emerge as productive alternatives or complements to political fervour. This is where euphoria emerges as a vital component of kinship work. Political kinship work, by its nature, connects us with others who we may not have found otherwise. It asks us to expand our horizon of solidarity, to see how our struggles interweave with those of others who have been relegated to the realm of 'wrong bodyminds', and ultimately to work towards forming extended (if not lifelong) relationships with those individuals and communities. Through this connective work between different 'wrong bodyminds', we inevitably discover more about what we have been told is impossible (Friedman, 2021). In relishing these novelties, marvelling at the expansion of our horizons, and heeding the call to reimagine our place in the world from 'wrong' to right, we are invited to find a liberatory euphoria that replenishes and reinvigorates us.

Political action is grim work. Political consciousness inevitably exposes us to the many vile depravities our increasingly fascistic world inflicts upon its citizens. One of the grimmest euphemisms to have emerged amongst activist circles over the past few months has been 'finding a work/life/genocide balance'. It is exactly this compartmentalization which barricades us away from euphoric kinship, and by extension meaningful kinship work. When we live a life where our jobs, our passions, and our political commitments are boxed away from one another, we deprive ourselves of the possibilities inherent in collapsing those walls. We painfully transition from one state to another, each a different type of betrayal to the others. This too is a type of dysphoria; any attempts to find a balance or compromise force us into states which are neither comfortable nor satisfactory, at best.

Euphoric kinship asks us to refuse compromise, and face the mounting heap of shit as well as the abundance that is on offer when we collapse these categories with the help of our kin. There is no 'work/life/genocide balance' in euphoric kinship because the machinations move outside of the realm of the individual. This approach not only offers us the relief of collective action and trust, but demands of us to engage in self-restoration as part of our political engagement. Euphoric kinship work is not centred around personal joy, but relief through collective work, and relishing in our personal efforts, no matter their perceived 'size'. Inertia and paralysis do not support radical change, but meaningful rest, facilitated by the mutuality of kinship, is central to our success (Hersey, 2022).

The Palestinian liberation movement's impact, particularly in Australia where the authors are based, once again provides us with concrete examples of long-lasting kinship work. Since Israel's escalation, the country has erupted in protests, direct actions, and other forms of resistance and support for the Palestinian people. But these actions have focused on more than political rage and anguish for those who are personally affected and their allies. Longer-term protests such as the Sit-Intifada (2024), which has been continuously running for well over 100 days at the time of writing, and the pro-Palestine sit-in outside Australian Prime Minister Anthony Albanese's office (SBS News, 2024), reveal what else is necessary to make a revolution work. Some people are there to go the distance and are focused on ensuring these protests are successful. Others provide food, come for short shifts to give longer-term protestors breaks, raise morale through art or conversation, or show up to provide a bigger presence and affirm their alignment with others in attendance. Euphoria does not exist in place of exhaustion, desperation, or frustration, but rather provides a central point we can reliably return to which provides an alternative to numbness, compartmentalization, or detachment. Euphoric kinship guarantees that we will have a time to revel in the richness of our shared lives, as it constantly reiterates the presence of community and others' commitment to that community. If the time to revel is not now, it is surely coming, and sometimes sooner than expected.

In this way, euphoric kinship attempts to transcend the misery/utopia binary discussed earlier in the chapter. But rather than denying either position, it harnesses both our protest screams and our utopic dreams and turns them into ecstasy, energy, fuel... We can either let our rage lead to despair or let it lead us forward. We can either use our passions to distract us or use them to better shape what a revolutionary life looks like for each of us. We have an option outside the bounds of fascist realism (Schmid, 2005), outside of living on the ever-thinning scraps of our oppressors. Revolutions can only be sustained across generations if euphoric, revolutionary ways of living are passed down. This is where all liberation struggles can not only intersect but interweave, if we extend our political horizons to see that the causes of all these oppressions are the very same culprits. We have to witness who is positioned as 'wrong' and whether they have been tarred by the same brush as we have. Racism, sexism, homophobia, transphobia; these are all exemplary subcategories of 'wrong bodyminds'.

Those who came before us[4] took risks not so we can sit comfortably, but so we can see that these risks are necessary for our collective survival. Our political elders have shown us not just the cost of resistance, but that it is worth every cent. There is no comfort, no connection, and most certainly no meaningful euphoria in a life divorced from these principles. The other side of this reality also rings true: there is comfort, connection, and meaning in connecting meaningfully with others, in truly immersing ourselves in a shared political reality.

This chapter is not advocating for sacrificing our individual needs for some perceived 'greater good'. Gender affirmation, disability access, and other fundamental needs which we are often deprived of (including housing, income stability, and so on) should not be put aside in service of a mythological, all-consuming Revolution. We have to live on. Many people (authors of this book included) cannot access what they would deem to be the necessary resources to achieve personal euphoria, or even a stable life. Yet, these same people are often found at the front line of revolutionary movements: cripples, transsexuals, queers, People of Colour, and highly targeted political dissidents across the anti-imperialist and anti-fascist left are driving liberation movements forward. Some may not last long, but those with access to political kinship are part of a system built to last. They

[4] And those still at it right now.

are doing it by the skin of their teeth, but they are not doing it alone. They are doing this work today because it is necessary, but also because it allows others to rest in preparation for tomorrow. They know that soon it will be their turn to rest.

## References


Alqaisiya, W. (2018). Decolonial queering: The politics of being queer in Palestine. *Journal of Palestine Studies, 47*(3), 29–44.

Carson, R. B. (2016). *Citizen body: The eugenical foundation of the United States and contemporary hauntings.* San Francisco State University Press.

Clapton, J., & Fitzgerald, J. (1997). The history of disability: A history of 'otherness'. *New Renaissance Magazine, 7*(1), 1–3.

Dominic, K. (2021). *The true transsexual and transnormativity: A critical discourse analysis of the wrong-body discourse.* PhD thesis,. University of British Colombia.

Friedman, M. (2021). On being impossible: Thoughts on ethnicity, embodiment and kinship. *Life Writing, 18*(3), 401–415.

Gazit, N. (2015). State-sponsored vigilantism: Jewish settlers' violence in the occupied Palestinian territories. *Sociology, 49*(3), 438–454.

Greaney, A.-M., & Flaherty, S. (2020). Self-care as care left undone? The ethics of the self-care agenda in contemporary healthcare policy. *Nursing Philosophy, 21*(1), e12291. https://doi.org/10.1111/nup.12291

Grech, S., & Soldatic, K. (2015). Disability and colonialism:(dis) encounters and anxious intersectionalities. *Social Identities, 21*(1), 1–5.

Gzesh, A. S. (2022). Queering kinship: Biopolitics, the death function, and transcendent capacity. *NEOS, 14*, 1–9.

Halberstam, J. (2016). Trans*-gender transitivity and new configurations of body, history, memory and kinship. *Parallax, 22*(3), 366–375.

Haraway, D. J. (2016). *Staying with the trouble: Making kin in the Chthulucene.* Duke University Press.

Hersey, T. (2022). *Rest is resistance: A manifesto.* Hachette UK.

Irving, D., Lewis, V., Bhanji, N., Connell, R., Driskill, Q., & Namaste, V. (2017). Trans* political economy deconstructed: A roundtable discussion. *TSQ, 4*(1), 16–27. https://doi.org/10.1215/23289252-3711505

Kafer, A. (2019). Crip kin, manifesting. *Catalyst: Feminism, Theory, Technoscience, 5*(1), 1–37.

Lake, R., & Dagostino, V. (2013). Converging self/other awareness: Erich Fromm and Paulo Freire on transcending the fear of freedom. In *Paulo Freire's intellectual roots: Towards historicity in praxis* (pp. 101–126). Continuum.

Legault, M., Bourdon, J.-N., & Poirier, P. (2021). From neurodiversity to neurodivergence: The role of epistemic and cognitive marginalization. *Synthese, 199*(5), 12843–12868.

Morris, B. (2018). *Kropotkin: The politics of community*. PM Press.

Quinn, H. (2023). Crip intimacy: Sockfriends, sexuality, and 'cripped things'. *Disability & Society, 1*, 1–22.

SBS News. (2024). 'He was one of us': Why this group stays overnight outside Anthony Albanese's office. *SBS News*. https://www.sbs.com.au/news/article/he-was-one-of-us-why-this-group-stays-overnight-outside-anthony-albaneses-office/968jqs9aa

Schmid, U. (2005). Style versus ideology: Towards a conceptualisation of fascist aesthetics. *Totalitarian Movements and Political Religions, 6*(1), 127–140.

Sedgwick, E. K. (2003). *Touching feeling*. Duke University Press.

Sit-Intifada. (2024, January 21). *The Sit-Intifada's substack*. https://thesitintifada.substack.com/

Sontag, S. (2013). *Illness as metaphor and AIDS and its metaphors*. Penguin UK.

Sullivan, N. (2008). The role of medicine in the (trans)formation of 'wrong' bodies. *Body & Society, 14*(1), 105–116. https://doi.org/10.1177/1357034X07087533

Taylor, S., & Gold, E. (2019). Madness and individualism: Unravelling in crazy times. In *Taboo transgression transcendence in art & science* (p. 135). Ionian University, Department of Audio and Visual Arts.

Thelen, T., & Alber, E. (2017). *Reconnecting state and kinship: Temporalities, scales, classifications*. University of Pennsylvania Press.

Wong, A. (2023, December 3). Why Palestinian liberation is disability justice. Disability Visibility Project. https://disabilityvisibilityproject.com/2023/12/02/why-palestinian-liberation-is-disability-justice/

CHAPTER 6

# Fucking Euphorically, Fucking Dysphorically

## Fucking Euphorically

You might find yourself thinking: 'isn't all fucking supposed to be euphoric?' We couldn't agree more, but we live in a world that is far from ideal. In fact, any attempts at naturalizing sex or reducing it to simplistic biological/psychological frameworks are naïve at best, and many such frameworks are ultimately oppressive in and of themselves. Regardless of whether a particular person or group wants to position sex as purely reproductive (read: 'natural'), or as an innately radical act,[1] inevitably fails to contend with the political and historical construction of how we identify sexuality, sexual pleasure, and the interaction of those factors with governments, oppressive lobbying groups, and the medical industrial complex (Tiefer, 2018). We cannot assume any one nature of sex: our experience and comprehension of sex is ultimately as multivalent and variable as the number of people who engage in it.

Sexual euphoria, particularly outside of trans circles, has been commodified by 'feminist' sexuality advocates, sex shops, and sex toy manufacturers (Huff, 2018). This erotic consumption is inevitably tied to capitalism[2] and furthers elitism and exclusivity around sexuality which

[1] This is particularly common amongst queers and other 'sex positivity' advocates.
[2] Boner killer.



S. Rosenberg et al., *The Trans Möbius Strip*, Critical and Applied Approaches in Sexuality, Gender and Identity,
https://doi.org/10.1007/978-3-031-70786-5_6

many of these influencers and companies claim to combat (Agoos, 2020). The emergence of packaged pleasure[3] is particularly impactful when we consider how pleasure capitalists have marketed our own orgasms to us as something beyond a bodily experience: they now form a part of a product-dependent identity which encircles around consumption of certain 'liberatory' items (Comella, 2017). Simultaneously, we can see how our sexual lives have also become a type of commodity, especially in terms of data mining in sex tech and related industries (Stardust et al., 2022). All of this is to say that many of us are being led down garden paths with regards to how pleasure, and by extent euphoria, can be understood and experienced within ourselves and with others.

We will use this chapter to explore the sexual possibilities that lie within a trans euphoria perspective, and to offer a counterpoint to other didactic framework for how sexual pleasure *should be*.[4] After all, we can now clearly see that the notion of simply fucking our way to liberation is just another way we are asked to silo ourselves and our 'private' aspects away from the greater tapestry of radical life which occurs outside the bedroom. If queer/trans sex was in itself liberatory, our world would be very different. This is why we need to look at sex as one tool amongst many that we must wield with awareness in order to achieve our liberatory goals, rather than concluding that the mere existence of queer sex is revolutionary. You need look no further than the downlow gay politicians who mow down pro-queer/trans policies or the closeted beat enthusiast-cum-gaybasher to know that the type of gendered sex someone has does not dictate the goodness of their impact on the world around them.

As discussed in other chapters, euphoria can be understood as something more than physiological or even emotional pleasure. Euphoria, in its most utopic sense, is that interconnection which reveals our porousness, our inevitable melding with others, and the transformative impact of that experience. Of course, the physiological and psychological components are also there; we are not selling any kind of transcendent Nirvana that you can access if you just think about it hard enough and attempt to circumvent your bodymind's material experience. Instead, we posit that euphoria can be felt most powerfully in the aftermath of events, in the connective tissue between disparate moments of pleasure and joy and satisfaction. An

[3] Or commodified cumming.

[4] E.g., Christianity, 'sexual liberation', Western tantra, whatever amorphous thing Andrea Dworkin was pushing for.

orgasm will often feel euphoric in the moment, but its *euphoric potential* lies beyond that moment.

While mainstream concepts of euphoria are most commonly explained through discussions of a supposed gender 'alignment' between our body and mind (we explore this further in other chapters), we can also supersede that dichotomy and explore the impact of a more metaphysical alignment. This alignment is what yields euphoria, harnessing euphoric potential through a coming-together of previously estranged aspects of ourselves. In the context of this chapter, this means we need to give further consideration both to the microscopic intimacies which can lead to euphoric experiences and the macroscopic aspects which affect our euphoric potential.

## Intimate (Counter-)Sexual Euphoria

Preciado (2018) gives us one example of a euphoric transformation within the intimate space. In their *Countersexual Manifesto*, Preciado suggests that the truly liberatory sexual potential within us exists in an experience that is divested from identities and relies entirely on the intensity and depth of interactions of specific bodies in time. He does this using dildos/phalluses as an extended metaphor, with vignettes and illustrations which place the 'symbolic' (e.g., a sex toy) against/inside the 'real' (e.g., human anatomy), forcing the reader to consider the false hierarchy we place on what is internal or external to our pleasure experience. It feels like Preciado's attempt at explaining why dykes and fags fuck each other, or why having one's silicon dildo sucked on can feel the same if not better than the 'real thing'. It is precisely this obsession with the 'real thing' which impedes access to sexual euphoria through the enforcement of hierarchical binaries such as flesh/silicon, coupledom/sluttiness, decent/dirty, straight/queer. Some of these 'unreal' things are still given a place in our life, but that place is restricted to bedrooms and other private areas, and its lower status is reasserted whenever these things get shoved back into our drawers or completely into the realm of our minds.

When we understand the deleterious effect of these false hierarchies we can begin the work of transcending them. Here Preciado's theory becomes more than just a philosophical thought exercise: he is encouraging us to use sex as a means of ascending rather than asserting our narratives of our bodyminds and identities. Fucking then becomes a technology of connection which can harness the power of momentary pleasures into something with more existential and longer-lasting consequences. In essence, while a good fuck is a good fuck, we can also access the euphoric potential of those experiences by witnessing our transitioning in and out of them and recognizing that the world does not stop at our bedroom door, nor can our bedroom experiences ever be entirely embargoed to our intimate spheres. Whether we admit to it or not, sex and sexual pleasure are woven into (and throughout) the tapestry of our lives, and always play a role in our evaluations of the world around us. This means that we expend energy on sexuality (ours and others') every single day. A euphoric perspective on sexuality is an invitation to reconsider where that energy is spent and the outcomes of repositioning ourselves in relation to both sexual pleasure and a higher goal of euphoria. We are invited to take the energy we would otherwise use to suppress and sharply define these experiences and instead put that same energy towards collective liberation and bodily as well as extrabodily connections.

## Euphoria and the Sexual Affective Atmosphere

Many of the sexual scripts we have to work to undo are manufactured by the opposite end of the spectrum to the most private and intimate—the sexual macrocosm which we all navigate. If euphoria at an inner world level is produced by refining and redefining pleasure and remoulding our bodily and extrabodily relationship to it, sexual euphoria at a macrocosmic level is where we can see how both euphoric and anti-euphoric narratives become collective realities. The sexual affective atmosphere (Anderson, 2009) which coats our lives is always in flux, and is as varied as the moments in space-time it affects. But there are broad currents that sweep across this landscape, clusters of lifestyles and ideologies which all vie for control over our individual and collective euphoric potential and its sexual technologies.

Rather than remaining in the realm of the abstract, it might benefit us to look at a case study. Consider SWERFs and their delicate positioning in relation to sexual pleasure. Many SWERFs identify as feminists, and push their anti-sex work rhetoric using a narrative of 'rescuing' (female) workers from a predatory (male-run) industry (Agustin, 2008). Through an imposition of one form of supposed liberation, SWERFs believe[5] they are helping our collective liberation. But even a cursory conversation with a

[5] Or at least claim to believe.

sex worker reveals the true intentions, or at the very least the consequences, of such 'liberation' work. Anti-sex worker campaigning and policymaking have further destabilized the industry, demonized both workers and clients, and pushed workers further into societal margins and socio-economic disadvantage. This is an ideology of relationality (it is, after all, an ideology about fucking) with significant consequences to broader society. SWERFs are certainly not keeping their bedroom behaviours contained to the family home, instead forcing their perspectives on workers and their communities. Hammes (2023) suggests that, in their attempts to cleanse human sexuality of evil, SWERFs have formed an ideology that is assembled around 'mistranslations of the radical potentialities of feminism' (Hammes, 2023, p. 52) which position all sexual labour as pro-rape, anti-woman, and innately anti-feminist human trafficking.

In the ideal 'liberated' world of the SWERF, sex could never be exchanged for money or be treated as transactional in any way. Fucking would be contained to the home,[6] and any discussions of it would undoubtedly have to be kept to a minimum outside the home in order to ensure no consent can be violated unintentionally. Very quickly you can see how the sexually ideal world of the SWERF starts feeling nearly as narrow as that of Christian fundamentalists or Hare Krishna. After all, SWERF logic follows many other repressive movements which position themselves as feminist or pro-woman despite finding the majority of sex abhorrent.[7] The same feminists who think sex workers are enemies to feminism tend to also condemn S/M (Merck, 2006), transness (Toone, 2018), as well as penetration writ large (Dworkin, 2008) for some of the more old-school 'political lesbians'. The people who hold these ideologies have not kept their worldviews in the private realm of their home. They are the people who oppose sex work decriminalization, trans healthcare, and many other realms of (trans)sexual liberation. This is as anti-euphoric as it gets: any semblance of divergence is met with punishment, and even the most static and still are rewarded with a pittance of what the human experience has to offer.

However, these ideologies are only effective in a vacuum, in the absence of counter-ideologies. Sex worker liberation, queer liberation, trans liberation, intersex liberation, and other human liberation movements continue to hold their ground and push for their version of the world to be born

[6] SWERFs are not particularly supportive of public sex (Dawthorne, 2018).

[7] See the band 108's tracks 'Woman' and 'Thorn' for some clarity on the Hare Krishna angle.

and reborn. Having seen an ideologically oppressive version of the world, we can now understand our role in worldbuilding, and how those aspects of our life we have been told to contain and secret away can have a radical impact. When our oppressors demand our silence, we have to scream. When our oppressors demand the status quo, we have to revolt. When our oppressors demand purity, we have to turn to filth.

In order to imagine this world, and how we can harness ourselves to bringing forth its existence, we need to understand the mechanisms of sexual euphoria. If repressive or anti-euphoric currents flow through our sexual affective atmosphere, we need to also identify some of the principles which we can cluster together into a coherent euphoric counter-ideology. In particular, we want to consider how we might connect with the transness inherent in sexual euphoria and utilize it as a means of materially, rather than just intellectually, bringing forth a revitalized and euphoric sexual landscape.

## The Axes of Trans-Sexual Euphoria

If we take the word trans at its most basic, it implies a shift from one space to another, from one era to the next. Trans sexual euphoria, then, is a call to trans[8] our understanding of sexual pleasure—to consider a method which explicates the principles of a euphoric sexuality and discerns it from more oppressive frameworks of sexuality. Many of these principles have already been crafted and polished for us, such as Mark Aguhar's (2012) axes:

1. Bodies are inherently valid
2. Remember death
3. Be ugly
4. Know beauty
5. It is complicated
6. Empathy
7. Choice
8. Reconstruct, reify
9. Respect, negotiate

These axes of queer/trans existence span across personal, interpersonal, and both future-facing and past-remembering aspects of our life. However,

[8] Read as a verb (Manion, 2020).

they are also intentionally broad, and are clearly designed as prompts rather than instructions. This intentional ambiguity results in there being many ways to interpret these axes and understand their intersections. We might benefit from a reconstruction of these principles based on the context we are discussing them in, or at least a consideration of these principles as we attempt to construct some axes for fucking euphorically.

1. *Our bodies are not always the centre of our pleasure*

Sometimes our bodies don't even need to be present for pleasure to occur. Sometimes our bodies must suffer so that others can experience pleasure. Sometimes our quest for bodily pleasure takes away from that of others. Sometimes pleasure is found in its denial. Sometimes your pleasure is completely irrelevant. Recognize these times, and your transitions through them.

2. *You are who/what you (recreationally) fuck*

We don't fuck cops, conservatives, TERFs, or any other people who stand in the way of liberation for all, at least not for free.[9] This is vital for three reasons: oppressors don't deserve pleasure; most fucking necessitates proximity which endangers us spiritually if not physically; and euphoria could never be found in a cradle of misery. Plus many of them are miserable lays no doubt.

3. *We can't fuck our way out of this*

If we always seek euphoria privately, it will always remain in the realm of the private. We need to expand our sense of liberatory euphoria beyond the bedroom, otherwise the 'revolution' is contained within those four walls. Very few intimate sexual encounters across history have yielded significant widespread material outcomes, and those that come to mind are disastrous to say the least.[10] We cannot fuck our way out of oppression, and our fucking is always experienced within an oppressive realm, whether we acknowledge it or not.

[9] The sacredness of sex work ultimately supersedes this point: when the choice is between fucking a cop or missing a rent payment, all bets are off.

[10] See: Bill Clinton's Wag the Dog comparisons (Dallek, 1998).

4. *Euphoria is earned*

Not only can euphoria not be bought, but it must be earned. Sexual euphoria is a cumulative experience, a process of weaving together our sexualities, bodyminds, and our position in a world we desire to radically change. Its payoff is not measured in orgasms or a high body count, but in the alignment we can begin to develop between our 'private' selves, our everyday movements, and the collective tapestry of euphoria (both sexual and non-sexual) that we are enmeshed in.

5. *Choose perversion*

When the choices presented to you are purity or perversion, choose perversion. The answer to suggestions of sexual modesty or moderation should never be acquiescence. Those who offer queer/trans perversity may challenge your palate, but those who offer innocence have much worse plans. In the same way there is no freedom without struggle, there is no freedom without disgust, overwhelm, terror, and other abhorrent emotional 'extremities' which a euphoric experience must contend with.[11]

6. *Euphoria withers where disconnection thrives*

We cannot be disconnected from our world, our kin, and our own deepest values and still experience what we are defining here as sexual euphoria. In the same way orgasms can occur in the absence of arousal or even consent, sexual pleasure too can exist at its maximum intensity without being euphoric. Sexual pleasure is transformed into sexual euphoria when the moment happens *within* the greater tapestry of revolution, rather than in the gaps that demarcate its *absence.*

7. *When in doubt, trans(ition)*

If euphoria is achieved through attenuation to greater forces, attenuation calls for developing our capacity to transition: from one headspace to another, from one relational context to another, from one lover to another. Whether a sexual encounter is T4T and/or faggy and/or dykey and/or Leathersex and so on is determined by how we trans ourselves to the

[11] We will discuss this more in the next section.

circumstances, and what the affect/effect of that transing is. We are already forced to trans(form) ourselves negatively, to subjugate ourselves to sexual scripts and bodily arrangements that we have no desire for. Sexual euphoria exists in that moment of conscious transition, in our refusal to make our fucking clinical or bourgeois or separate from our broader liberation struggles.

8. *The sexual revolution will not be commodified*

As we stated above, euphoria is *earned*, not bought, and euphoric sexual liberation can never come from factories, retailers, or 'sex positive' microcelebrities with corporate sponsorships. It is important to understand that when we say the sexual revolution will not be commodified, we are not implying that sex toys or transactional sex will cease to exist. In fact, workers and worker-run spaces exist in diametric opposition to these mass-production and hyper-commodification industries, and can craft experiences of sexual euphoria more powerfully and skilfully than most of us could even imagine. Ultimately, euphoria can be facilitated by a product or paid sexual services, but our responsibility for (co-)creating it can never be taken away.

## Fucking Dysphorically

It may seem a contradiction to even discuss the notion of fucking dysphorically. After all, we are told that gender dysphoria gets in the way of sexuality (Bartolucci et al., 2015; Cerwenka et al., 2014; Martin & Coolhart, 2022), and that it is ultimately a negative experience that must be banished for euphoria to be experienced. However, as we discussed in previous chapters, a total absence of dysphoria is an ideal that arguably no one reaches. We therefore cannot look away from dysphoria or harness our efforts entirely to the project of its suppression.

Questioning the truthfulness of many 'euphoric' promises also has the potential to unveil the falsity of many 'dysphoric' warnings. In other words, if euphoria has been reduced down to detached pleasure, then dysphoria has also been reduced down to abject suffering. If euphoria provides us a lens on sexual pleasure which refocuses us towards greater experiences, dysphoria as a lens shows that those 'darker' sides of our sexuality can be repositioned and reconsidered.

As mentioned in the axes we discussed above, sexual perversion can provide a vital entry point to a sexuality beyond commodification, puritanism, and homogeneity. We want to make a distinction here between sexual perversion par excellence and BDSM. While BDSM can be understood as a sexual revolutionary movement, many of its proponents have also succumbed to pressures of respectability and legibility from the mainstream (Weiss, 2008). Like other sexual identities, BDSM describes a cluster of sexual behaviours, but the euphoric potential of those sexual technologies lies beyond the impact[12] of the actions themselves. We can't spank and shibari ourselves out of our political reality any more than we can fuck our way out.

However, as with the euphoric sexual technologies we have discussed in this chapter, seemingly dysphoric sexual affects can also produce atmospheres and experiences which have a euphoric potential. Dysphoria is a narrative that frames all negative experiences as noxious weeds that need to be removed. The fundamental emotions of dysphoria are humiliation, degradation, pain, isolation, and psychophysical bondage.[13] These oppressive experiences, viewed entirely through the simplified binary of euphoria as fundamentally positive and dysphoria as fundamentally negative, are perpetually excised or pushed down within ourselves. In contrast to this perspective, a euphoric sexual perversion approach takes many of the fundamental aspects of dysphoria and funnels their energy into more fruitful experiences.

This is not a new perspective: BDSM, Leathersex, and other forms of sexual perversion have always provided a guiding light to those who sought these experiences (Antolovich, 1994). Sexually perverse acts, when enacted within a radical trans sexual framework, can become reclamations and disaffirmations of the very things we have been told are most destructive to our well-being (Zahn, 2018). This is doubly true for trans sexual perverts, for whom gender transgression and sexual transgression exist beyond the binaries of good/bad, suffering/joy, permitted/forbidden (Kaldera, 2009). Both perversion and dysphoria rely on a certain type of narrative distortion, the former usually happening voluntarily while the other is often foisted upon us. After all, there is no 'truth' to the stories dysphoria tells us about ourselves; it is merely a reflection of broader

[12] Pun intended.

[13] See Chap. 3's discussion of euphoria in the absence of gender-affirming medical care access.

distorted narratives around which bodies are appropriate for which genders. Dysphoria reflects the monstrous nature of colonial history and its destruction of non-normative, non-binary gender expressions. Perversion, on the other hand, erupts from the same narrative fount, but materializes in radically different ways.

Where a directly dysphoric narrative might position parts of your body or self as existing in misalignment with your core self, a perverted dysphoric narrative asks what can be done about those material realities beyond simple repression or a (sometimes literal) cutting away of the concerning matter. If you haven't cut off your tits, what can you do with them beyond tucking them away? If you have kept your cock, can it play a role in your life despite its misalignment? If you're a trans woman, can you still be a Daddy? Fucking dysphorically[14] means recognizing negative narratives about your body and, as we have already said, choosing perversion. The simple and pure approach would require you to put those uncomfortable parts away, to sequester them and treat them as issues to be solved at a later date. Fucking dysphorically invites you to find other things amongst those negative experiences, to probe your comfort zone and consider which aspects of your dysphoria are crucial and which impede both the most intimate and most holistic aspects of your life.

The euphoric potential of fucking dysphorically lies not only in eroticizing experiences such as humiliation (Kali, 2017), but in understanding the transformative power of that subversion, and finding out where else to apply it. If we can recomprehend pain, suffering, and degradation within the intimate realm, we can also begin to understand how those reimaginings can flow beyond the bedroom. Through a euphoric perverted lens we are given the opportunity to see that our pain and anguish are not only caused by external or internal afflictions but also by our devotion, discipline, and meaningful sacrifice to something greater than us. If pain and fear can be transmogrified in such a radical way within intimate contexts, you can clearly see how this might transfer to other aspects of life. Suddenly the policeman, the Christian fanatic, the hateful politician, all have the sting taken out of their presence. A defiant, curious, and euphoric perspective provides us with an opportunity to pervert the power dynamics at play. If these people and groups want us to cower, we stand up straighter.

[14] Which is to say, fucking despite the presence of internal turmoils around gender and embodiment.

If their demands for a heterosexual morality attempt to silence us, we scream louder. If their physical and stochastic violence is meant to deter us, we push back even harder.

If fucking euphorically is about ensuring our sexuality does not become separated from the rest of our life and the world around us, fucking dysphorically is about ensuring our sexuality (and by extension our whole existence) does not become defined by purity and perfection at the cost of its intriguing complexity and fullness. In both cases, the euphoric potential of these modalities is defined not by any momentary pleasure, but rather by how these experiences transform us, and how they can remain connected to our politics and worldviews. These are not solutions to dysphoria or any kind of guide on better sex. Instead, this chapter has aimed to explore the outer edges of both euphoria and dysphoria, and to question the stability and viability of the euphoria/dysphoria binary from its most intimate to its most universal implications.

## References

Agoos, E. (2020). Women's erotic consumption: Articulating the sexual self under late capitalism. *Inquiries Journal, 12*(07) http://www.inquiriesjournal.com/articles/1785/womens-erotic-consumption-articulating-the-sexual-self-under-late-capitalism

Aguhar, M. (2012). These are the axes [Tumblr]. *Tumblr.* https://markaguhar.tumblr.com/post/17806858973/these-are-the-axes-1-bodies-are-inherently

Agustin, L. M. (2008). *Sex at the margins: Migration, labour markets and the rescue industry.* Bloomsbury Publishing.

Anderson, B. (2009). Affective atmospheres. *Emotion, Space and Society, 2*(2), 77–81.

Antolovich, G. (1994). Living in leather: An inner journey. In M. Thompson (Ed.), *Leather-folk, radical sex, people, politics and practice* (pp. 252–256). Alyson Publications.

Bartolucci, C., Gómez-Gil, E., Salamero, M., Esteva, I., Guillamón, A., Zubiaurre, L., Molero, F., & Montejo, A. L. (2015). Sexual quality of life in gender-dysphoric adults before genital sex reassignment surgery. *The Journal of Sexual Medicine, 12*(1), 180–188.

Cerwenka, S., Nieder, T. O., Cohen-Kettenis, P., De Cuypere, G., Haraldsen, I. R. H., Kreukels, B. P., & Richter-Appelt, H. (2014). Sexual behavior of gender-dysphoric individuals before gender-confirming interventions: A European multicenter study. *Journal of Sex & Marital Therapy, 40*(5), 457–471.

Comella, L. (2017). *Vibrator nation: How feminist sex-toy stores changed the business of pleasure.* Duke University Press.

Dallek, R. (1998, August 21). Are Clinton's bombs wagging the dog? *Los Angeles Times*. https://www.latimes.com/archives/la-xpm-1998-aug-21-me-15131-story.html

Dawthorne, N. (2018). *Intelligible variability: Narratives of male sex work in London Ontario Canada*.

Dworkin, A. (2008). *Intercourse*. Basic Books.

Hammes, A. (2023). SWERF Necropolitics: Three sites of feminist mistranslation and the politics of feminist exclusion. *Journal of Feminist Scholarship, 23*(23), 52–69. https://doi.org/10.23860/jfs.2023.23.05

Huff, A. (2018). Liberation and pleasure: Feminist sex shops and the politics of consumption. *Women's Studies, 47*(4), 427–446. https://doi.org/10.1080/00497878.2018.1454923

Kaldera, R. (2009). *Double edge: The intersections of transgender and BDSM*. Alfred Press.

Kali, P. (2017). *Enough to make you blush: Exploring erotic humiliation workbook*. Erotication Publications.

Manion, J. (2020). *Female husbands: A trans history*. Cambridge University Press.

Martin, T. K., & Coolhart, D. (2022). "Because your dysphoria gets in the way of you…it affects everything." The mental, physical, and relational aspects of navigating body dysphoria and sex for trans masculine people. *Sexual and Relationship Therapy, 37*(1), 82–99. https://doi.org/10.1080/14681994.2019.1696459

Merck, M. (2006). The feminist ethics of lesbian sadomasochism. In *Perversion*. Routledge.

Preciado, P. B. (2018). *Countersexual manifesto*. Columbia University Press.

Stardust, Z., Kennedy, J., & Albury, K. (2022). *Public interest sex tech hackathon: Speculative futures and participatory design (Australia) [Report]*. ARC Centre of Excellence for Automated Decision-Making and Society, Queensland University of Technology, RMIT University, Swinburne University of Technology. https://apo.org.au/node/318398

Tiefer, L. (2018). *Sex is not a natural act & other essays*. Routledge.

Toone, K. (2018). Come back for us: A critical reflection on the shared history of queers and sex workers and our need for solidarity. *Hecate, 44*(1/2), 110–121.

Weiss, M. (2008). Gay shame and BDSM pride: Neoliberalism, privacy, and sexual politics. *Radical History Review, 100*, 87. https://doi.org/10.1215/01636545-2007-023

Zahn, R. (2018). *Productive paddles and productive power: An exploration of transgender individuals' negotiation of identity through BDSM practices*. Minnesota State University.

PART III

# Euphoria-Forward Approaches

CHAPTER 7

# Relational Euphoria: Fractures and Healing

## Introduction

Families are fraught places for many people. Family dynamics can be loving, supportive, and safe, they can be abusive, cold, and rejecting, and they can of course be a mixture of both. For trans peoples, family dynamics can be heightened as a result of cisgenderism. This can include family members simply not understanding what it means to be trans, and taking their own time to process and come to a place of understanding. It can also include family members who are very understanding, but who in their rush to be affirming may reinforce transnormative tropes. And sadly, for many trans peoples families can also resort to what Rogers (2017) refers to as 'honour-based abuse', where trans peoples are seen as bringing shame to families, leading family members to be hostile, abusive, and to reject trans peoples.

In this chapter we explore fractures that occur in families following a family member disclosing that they are trans, but we also explore how, through relationships, healing can occur in both the broader and familial context of cisgenderism. Thinking through the figure of the trans Möbius strip, and following the work of Foucault (2008), we can usefully think of families as nodes through which individuals are made from the social. As we outlined in Chap. 1, and drawing on the work of the Curt collective



S. Rosenberg et al., *The Trans Möbius Strip*, Critical and Applied Approaches in Sexuality, Gender and Identity,
https://doi.org/10.1007/978-3-031-70786-5_7

(1994), individuals are formed as nodes of the social. Families constitute a key site where this occurs: discourses about what it means to be a person, be a gender, be morally good, and so forth, are all intimately shaped through our familial relationships. Further, not only do families shape who we are within a relationship to hegemonic discourses of the self, but they also serve as points of insertion into a normative social order, regulating who we can and cannot be.

Just as much as our families shape us, we can (re)shape our families. To suggest this is not to employ the simplistic understanding often evident in literature on trans people and our families, namely, that families are 'transformed' by including a trans person. This type of neoliberal inclusion more often than not emphasizes the changes supposedly forced upon families by trans people, and often translates into simplistic accounts of 'better understanding diversity' and 'being inclusive'. Instead, in this chapter we explore what it means to think about trans peoples as radical agents of change within the context of families (here referring to both our chosen families and our nuclear families). Importantly, this is not to suggest that it is the duty of trans peoples to serve as such agents, nor that such agency is always effective in creating change. Rather, our suggestion is that trans peoples, through our being, often resist the normative imposition of familial rules.

## Disharmony, Harm, and Fractures in Families

While we are seeking to avoid damage-centred accounts in this book, we would be remiss if we did not speak about the harms caused to trans peoples by our families. Harms can occur when families struggle to accept us when we tell them we are trans. Some family members—and in particular parents and grandparents—often tell us that they need time to understand, placing a burden on us to help them to understand. This is often the best case scenario for many trans peoples. While, with a generosity of spirit, we can help our families move to a place of understanding, this is not without cost. Often we must tolerate misgendering for a considerable period of time, in order to facilitate family members and not push them away. This is a burden for trans peoples, make no mistake.

Yet the burden of supporting family members to eventually support us is often not the most salient framing of the situation. All too often both anecdotally, in the media, and in academic writing, the language of 'loss' is deployed, and indeed the language of 'ambiguous loss'. Ambiguous loss typically refers to a loss that is difficult to grieve. This can be when someone is present but absent: such as for people living with dementia. The person is present, but may not remember us. Ambiguous loss can also occur when someone is no longer present, but when we do not know where they are. This can be when a person has been reported missing and is not found. Certainly, some trans people live with dementia, and sadly given the high rates of abuse and murder of trans peoples, some trans people 'go missing'. But neither of these are what is meant when people refer to trans people and ambiguous loss. Instead, what is meant is that family members feel that they are mourning the loss of a previously assumed gender, but given the person is still there, they struggle to mourn.

Have no doubt, this language of loss, grief, and mourning is harmful to trans peoples. To say that we are an object to grieve contributes to the framing of us living unintelligible lives, lives that are being lived while other people are grieving them. Again, this places a burden on trans peoples to support others to support us. A focus on claims to loss also place a burden on us to show that we haven't changed. The narrative of 'my gender has changed but I am still the same person' is a transnormative trope often expected of us as a salve to our family members. Yet this belies that for many trans people living as our gender constitutes a fundamental change in our ways of being, our understanding of ourselves, and our relationships with others. To appease others by telling them we are just the same person does a disservice to our transness.

This language of loss is often also evident when it comes to our intimate partners. Certainly, we acknowledge that our intimate partners face change when we transition in the context of an existing relationship. Yet all relationships face change: it is a constant. It is absolutely true that our partners may need to adjust how they think about us, themselves, and the relationship, but this constitutes an opportunity for growth and change, not a loss. The language of loss only makes sense when we see sameness as the goal: that we remain the same person doing the same things in the same ways across time. Locking ourselves and others into an expectation of sameness is a pathway to stagnation and resentment. We are not 'dishonouring' our families by living our transness. Rather, we are both honouring ourselves, and dishonouring cisgenderist discourses that serve to regulate and control us all.

## Growth, Change, and Euphoric Alliances

Before we proceed to consider the potential for change in families, it is important that we make something very clear. Trans peoples should not be or feel compelled to be agents of change. It is not our moral duty to help cis people. Normative moral accounts of family would claim that above all else, family should be honoured, protected, and adhered to. Yet it is precisely such accounts of family that do us harm. Trans peoples are entitled to walk away from family forever, to take space from family to consider our relationship to our family, and we are of course entitled to lovingly embrace and be lovingly embraced by our family. This is our decision to make, guided by our own assessments and experiences.

While it is certainly true that posttraumatic growth is possible for trans peoples in all aspects of our lives, we must also be mindful of the trauma. We don't experience posttraumatic growth without trauma. And if the source of that trauma is our family, well while we might appreciate aspects of the growth and resilience that takes place, that doesn't mean we have to forgive or forget the trauma caused by our families. Choosing to engage with our families is something we can agree to or rescind at any time. If we choose to engage with our families (including our nuclear families, our chosen families, and our intimate partners), it is important that we set the terms of the engagement, as much as we are respectful of the fact that relationships are constituted by more than one person. We must know our own boundaries and limits for engagement, what constitutes a no for us, what we might be willing to entertain, tolerate, or accept, and how we will monitor all of this going forward.

As agents of change, trans peoples can usefully think about all interactions in which we take part through the lens of relationship flags. A red flag, for example, might be someone being purposively abusive towards us. This is something we would hope to walk away from, quickly. We know that there are many factors that keep trans people in abusive relationships: financial control, threats to out someone, threats of harm to ourselves and our loved ones (both human and non-human), and past experiences of abuse that lead us to believe that it is all we deserve. We are not simplistically suggesting that trans people can always easily walk away from abuse. What we are suggesting, however, is that trans people are entitled to walk away, and that it is trans people who determine what counts as abuse, not our abusers.

Yellow flags are those things that might serve as a reminder to us to keep an eye on patterns or behaviours in our relationships with others. A yellow flag might be a family member who on the surface appears to accept our transness, but who misgenders us long after we have told them our name and pronouns, and despite regular reminders. We might choose to speak with this person and explore why this is happening. We might ask another person to intervene on our behalf. Or ultimately we might choose to take some space from that person. A yellow flag is not an automatic injunction to act, including to leave (though it might come to constitute that). Rather, a yellow flag is a reminder to us to watch, and to be guided by our feelings and to see our feelings as legitimate.

And of course there are green flags. Green flags are the things that other people do in their relationship with us that enable us to feel seen and heard. It might be someone speaking up for us. It might be someone educating someone else, instead of us doing the work. It might just be someone loving us for who we are. These are things that should be part of any caring relationship, and trans people should expect no less. Indeed, it is sad that these things should even need to be named as green flags. Unfortunately, given cisgenderism, green flags can be rare for some trans peoples in our relationships with others, so it is important to recognize them. For sure, no one is expected to be perfect. Trans peoples are entitled to mourn our losses: of friendships, relationships, and family. But also important is that we celebrate the joys we experience brought by our relationships with other people. Celebrating relationship joys can complement the joys we experience by being ourselves.

Importantly, we want to emphasize here that the role of family in celebrating our joys is not limited to our human kin. Our animal companions too can play an important role in sharing in our joys. Indeed, our research has found that animal companions are often perceived as offering non-judgmental support to trans peoples, but further that relationships with animal companions can provide us as trans people with ways to think beyond the human in terms of what counts as kinship and relationships (Skelton & Riggs, 2024). In the face of hostility animals provide us with support, and they do so on their own terms, rather than bringing with them a human lens. This does not mean that animals are a blank slate: they will have their own ways of judging us. For example, we have discussed how animals may notice when we start hormone therapy, and that may change how they interact with us (Riggs et al., 2021). Nonetheless, animal ways of being stand in stark contrast to human ways of being (that may often be cisgenderist), and can be an important source of support for trans people.

In terms of our human families, what can they do, alongside us, to create space for euphoria? One answer to this is not to rely upon neoliberal understandings of inclusion. Bluntly praising us on our appearance, or demonstrating to us their use of pronouns, is not likely to be euphoria-inducing. As humans, trans peoples should be allowed to expect positive regard: it should not be exceptional and praiseworthy. By contrast, euphoric alliances are those where our cis family members, friends, and intimate partners are willing to be accomplices in fighting back against cisgenderism. For example, our parents might support and endorse us refusing to engage with family members who are not supportive. Indeed, they might well prioritize their loving relationships with us over relationships with problematic family members. Our accomplices will be both led by us, while also taking the lead. They will listen to our stated needs, while also not relying upon us to educate them. They will move beyond us being the token trans person in their village, to developing a depth, relational understanding of transness.

A euphoric relationship is not one where all parties get it right all of the time. This is an unrealistic expectation. Instead, euphoric relationships are those built on trust about intent: intent to love without cisgenderist conditions, intent to support and fight together, and intent to engage in genuine capacity building, rather than simply propping up unjust structures. And this applies to all relationships. Trans people don't automatically know the needs of other trans people, even if our insider knowledges might provide us with some leverage. But a euphoric relationship is one that starts from the place of positive mutual regard, and seeks to explore the needs and desires of all parties.

## Concluding Thoughts

In suggesting that trans peoples can be radical agents of change in the context of families, our argument is relatively simple: by refusing to accept the moral injunction that families must be preserved above all else, we refuse to be inserted into normative discourses about family specifically, and social inclusion more broadly. Instead, we choose, when we can, to prioritize our own needs, which can include walking away from some of our family, and creating our own chosen families. These are indeed all choices: choices that trans peoples are entitled to make, and which are not arbitrary nor are they based on a whim. Rather, given our unfortunately depth knowledge of cisgenderism, we are well placed to know which relationships work for us, and which do not. For some trans peoples this may take time. Time to understand the harms caused to us, time to understand that we do not deserve harm.

When we think about trans peoples and family, then, we cannot restrict out thinking to individual interactions. Rather, we must always think about family through the lens of the trans Möbius strip. How are families both potential sites of euphoric alliances, and also points of insertion into a normative social order. How do families provide opportunities for growth for all parties, as also serving a normative regulatory moral order. When we work with the concept of relationship flags, we can be better placed to see when any given relationship is not working for us and why, and to make decisions that prioritize our own safety. Our cis loved ones can be part of this journey towards safety, but only if they are willing to do the work required of walking alongside us.

## References

Curt, B. C. (1994). *Textuality and tectonics: Troubling social and psychological science*. Open University Press.

Foucault, M. (2008). *Psychiatric power: Lectures at the College de France, 1973–1974* (Vol. 1). Macmillan.

Riggs, D. W., Rosenberg, S., Fraser, H., & Taylor, N. (2021). *Queer entanglements: Intersections of gender, sexuality, and animal companionship*. Cambridge University Press.

Rogers, M. (2017). Transphobic 'honour'-based abuse: A conceptual tool. *Sociology, 51*(2), 225–240.

Skelton, S., & Riggs, D. W. (2024). Exploring the more-than-human in trans people's lives: Connections, sociality, being and animal companionship. *International Journal of Transgender Health*, 1. Online First.

CHAPTER 8

# The Imagined Transpolitic and the Transsexual Intifada: Euphoria, Dysphoria, and Political Action

## Introduction

Contemporary mainstream discourse around transness has undergone a significant transformation over the past couple of decades. As part of the 'trans tipping point', a spectre which we suspect will haunt us for a long time, words like 'acceptance' and 'embracing' have become increasingly dominant in discussions of the trans cause. These are in stark contrast to the dominant language surrounding transness at the turn of the century and further back: trans people were not acceptable or embraced, but monstrous, pitiable, disgusting. For many the 'tipping point' was an understandably welcome change—after all, existentially speaking, it is better to be (uncomfortably) embraced than actively reviled. But with this shift in cis people's perspective on transness and trans people came an inevitable softening of how trans politics were understood both by the world and our communities.

This softening is part of a process that has already been at work for some time: transnormativity. Transnormativity, like heteronormativity or cisnormativity, implies a kind of bridling of trans politics. It is a compartmentalizing process which dissects trans life, rescuing what is considered 'vital' and relegating other parts to waste. The survivors of this dissection are those things which are easiest to assimilate: our art, our image, and our



S. Rosenberg et al., *The Trans Möbius Strip*, Critical and Applied Approaches in Sexuality, Gender and Identity,
https://doi.org/10.1007/978-3-031-70786-5_8

personal stories of grief and hurt. After all, we make/are beautiful things, but we must also remain positioned as ever-suffering, as a kind of penance for our genius and uniquity. This image of an 'acceptable' trans person has been perfectly moulded, but we can learn more from what has been discarded than we can from final sculpture. The parts of transness which have been cast aside contain everything that could not be subsumed into the mainstream, into the realm of the socially acceptable, into inoffensive and monetizable slices of 'trans life'. They contain the essence of a transpolitical existence, which sits in direct opposition to transnormativity's *Imagined Transpolitic.* The sanitized image of transness that we are exposed to on our black mirrors and in so-called trans-inclusive centrist/liberal spaces is an indictment on the state of trans politics today.

## The Imagined Transpolitic

Beyond 'gender-affirming' and policy-obsessed media, outside of happy-clappy 'pride' centres and inner suburb Rainbow Ticked cafes, in the realm of the general public, we are met with a very different political landscape to what the Imagined Transpolitic dictates. The Imagined Transpolitic waves a 'mission accomplished' banner, Bush Junior-era irony included (LINDSAY, 2011), declaring trans peoples' political goals to be largely fought-for and won. There are a few vestiges of trans rights which remain open battlegrounds, in particular around matters of trans peoples' presence in public bathrooms, sports, linguistics, and mass media. These are the arenas in which the Imagined Transpolitic tells us our fights must be fought. The Imagined Transpolitic places its lot with lobbying, with 'good faith' philanthropism, with an allyship that asks us to change ourselves 'just a little' for the sake of others' comfort the same way we are asking cisgender people for 'just a little' more basic humanity. In essence, the Imagined Transpolitic is an intentionally counter-revolutionary ideology which replaces trans collective struggle with well-crafted ideals of personal achievement. This position is truly imagined, in the sense that it is entirely reliant on images and their reorientation.

The mirage of the Imagined Transpolitic relies on the same principles as the illusory desert oasis: it materializes in moments of sheer desperation, and offers an alluringly simple solution to a deeply existential issue. Like the mirage of the oasis, the Imagined Transpolitic claims to be nourishing, to give us what we have been deprived of most. Like the mirage of the oasis, the Imagined Transpolitic is both opaque and superficial, a seemingly concrete image that travels away from you as fast as you travel towards it, or allows you to pass through it like a veil of smoke, leaving you with nothing in hand. Like the mirage of the oasis, we find ourselves parched no matter how close we get to that miraculous sight. The Imagined Transpolitic, that cluster of political issues we have been told are the sum of trans politics, is nothing but a spectre. It is an intentionally empty promise.

## The Imagined Transpolitic: Actors, Methods, Goals

Like any zealous propaganda campaign, the Imagined Transpolitic represents the desires of a select few within a broader populace it claims to represent. This fictional political narrative clearly holds less-than-liberatory ideals at heart, which becomes clearer once we investigate its proponents, methods, and goals. Transnormativity and the Imagined Transpolitic's advocates take many forms: celebrities and other wealthy trans people who flaunt and laud their upper-class access to surgeries and other forms of gender-affirming transformations; transgender advocates (regardless of gender) who reject solidarity and intersectional politics and prioritize trans issues above all others; transgender capitalists and their corporations, businesses, and NGOs, who rely on trans misery for their continued existence; gender-affirming specialists and surgeons who would never willingly have a trans person in their home; gender studies academics who value intellectual work over direct engagement and use trans lives for their own financial and career interests; and others whose vision of trans rights is wafer-thin and kept entirely within the realm of capitalist, individualist, colonialist frameworks. In addition to these, of course, is the inevitable trickle-down into the broader public, who have internalized these elitist mentalities and uphold these people and institutions as beacons of trans progress.

If we can understand that these are the people and groups pushing for an intentionally myopic, narrow, and neutered form of a transpolitic, then we also need to understand their methods. The Imagined Transpolitic, intellectual and disembodied by nature, resides largely in the realm of media, marketing, policy, and the medical and academic industrial complexes. We are sold the Imagined Transpolitic when we are asked to applaud the surgically induced 'trans joy' (McNamara, 2023; Ring, 2023;

Wratten, 2023) or the supposedly superior intellect of the wealthy,[1] to supplant our personal needs in favour of idolizing bourgeoisie outliers to the trans experience, and to obsess with trans narratives we will never have access to. We are also asked to pity these proponents of the Imagined Transpolitic when they receive fallout, and to spend our precious time and energy supporting these individuals when the 'culture wars' inevitably consume them. There is a method at play here, a strategy that not only orientates its target audience towards unachievable life goals and sponsored content, but also sharply turns them away from radical politics and the lived reality of trans peoples outside of the ivory tower.

All these attention-grabbing invitations may seem disparate or too fleeting to investigate, or alternatively they might just blend into the broader swamp of for-profit mass media overload most of us are harnessed to daily (Vorderer et al., 2017). Both of these perspectives exist by design. Either way, these messages have burrowed into the subconscious tapestry of our everyday culture, and made themselves subtle fixtures in the conversations, media, and political discourse we engage with daily. These methods operate the same whether they are applied interpersonally, bureaucratically, or artistically. Like a transgender Hasbara (Aouragh, 2016), the Imagined Transpolitic thrives through repetition rather than evolution. The messages are set in stone, and in many ways have not evolved much over the past century. They are messages which push notions of purity, simplicity, acceptability, conformity, and gratitude for what morsels we have been given over the decades. The latter is particularly pertinent, and hints towards the goals that the Imagined Transpolitic holds when it comes to our personal, collective, and political lives as trans peoples.

When we are being sold conventional trans beauty we are asked to look away from butchness, from genderfucking, from 'bricks', and from any other outliers that would suggest you can live in whatever body you want to and thrive as a trans person. When we are being sold reductive and single-issue trans politics we are asked to look away from complexity, from intersectional solidarity outside the gates of transness, and perhaps most importantly we are being asked to look away from our own complicity in mechanisms of oppression. When we are being sold a trans life where you could almost seamlessly exist without your transness being in focus, we are being asked to look away from the power of the 'trans shock factor', from

[1] Whether they are actors, academics, old money, etc.

our profound gender uniquity and transsexual courage, and from the many aspects of ourselves that are perfect in their Holiness, viscerality, innovation, and/or perversion. We are asked to leave so much behind, in favour of so little. These repressive political mechanisms ultimately 'thrive on the disavowal, theft, and destruction of our ways of life, and of our dreams' (Gill-Peterson, 2024).

The goals of this intentional curtailing of trans potential, of the creation and maintenance of the Imagined Transpolitic, are similarly targeted at all aspects of our lives. The Imagined Transpolitic serves to keep the radical implications of transness contained. It wants transness to remain a medical condition in need of treatment, rather than, as the Vatican recently put it, a way to 'make oneself G-d' (Al Jazeera, 2024). It wants transness to always feel a little wrong and a little tragic, rather than understanding transness as a core human experience that has been vilified for centuries, and that those vilifiers deserve comeuppance, not comradery. It wants 'peace' between trans peoples and cisgender people, not trans justice, which will inevitably necessitate unrest and discomfort (at the very least) amongst the cisgender population. The existence of transness in an oppressive, gender binary world is not a tokenistic charity case: it is an apocalypse, an anarchist revolution, an Intifada.

## The Transsexual Intifada

Revolution and Intifada in the context of queerness are not new concepts. Anderson (2015) discusses how an Intifada within the realm of 'LGBT' activism focuses on more than just social acceptability within Western paradigms; rather, a revolution/Intifada in queerness requires a critical position on and practical approach to the role that colonialism, Western expansionism, globalization, and racialized geopolitics play in shaping how we understand things such as gender and sexuality as distinct categories. Here we can again take lessons from Palestine, in particular Palestine's Unity Intifada. This framework shows the decolonilizing structures which underpin the concept of Intifada, and highlights the roles of diverse communities (including queers and trans peoples) in bringing forward a holistic counterpoint to fascistic, colonizing forces and ideologies (Alqaisiya, 2023).

As Herman (2015) points out, there is a vital distinction between viewing transness as innately revolutionary and understanding the 'methods' of transness as opportunities for revolutionary praxis. The Imagined

Transpolitic wants us to think that trans people are revolutionary by their mere existence. This position seeks to neutralize us, to make us believe that we are just as revolutionary when we consume trans media in our homes as we could be if we took direct action against our oppressors, whether they are Christian lobbyists, career TERFs, liberal rainbow orgs, politicians, governments, or medical institutions. Our inner lives cannot centre around complacency and individualistic survival without having adverse political and material impacts on others. The Imagined Transpolitic wants us at home, at a party, or in a movie theatre. It is distinctly designed to deter us from going to the homes of the wealthy, the picket line, or the factory barricade. If radical transness teaches us that our suffering is the result of systemic transphobic oppression, then a transsexual Intifada teaches us that these intersecting systems of control extend far beyond gender oppression, and that our daily political lives must reflect that reality.

It's important to note that the Imagined Transpolitic is not omnipresent or all-engulfing. Examples of radical, principled trans actions abound, especially within anti-war and anti-imperialist activism. Slogans such as "mones not drones' and 'war profiteers kill queers' (Queer Trans War Ban, 2024) have been established as regular rallying cries at political demonstrations and direct actions. Since 7 October, radical Intifada solidarity between trans peoples and Palestinians[2] seems to have skyrocketed. 'Queers for Palestine' and 'Trans People for Palestine' groups are emerging across the Western world, further reinforcing the vital relationship between queer/trans liberation and the struggle for freedom at a global scale. Perhaps one of the most controversial trans-related Intifada acts to have made it into the mainstream media was Aaron Bushnell's immolation in front of the Israeli embassy in protest of the Palestinian genocide (Pierpont, 2024). Since their death, information has emerged through online trans networks that seems to suggest Aaron was consistently identifying as Lilly (or LillyAnarKitty in online forums) for some time prior to her fatal protest (Urquhart, 2024). While we will never have a full picture, we can still see that Lilly/Aaron's life involved both transness *and* forward, holistic political engagement. We are not claiming that Lilly/Aaron's self-immolation was caused by her transness, but rather that it was through her transness that she found more expansive politics, which

[2] As well as other communities who have experienced renewed military assaults by the Zionist entity.

transformed her not only in terms of gender experience but in terms of her relationship to the US military industrial complex and its complicity in the Palestinian genocide. Lilly/Aaron should be with us today, fighting alongside us. But she made an ultimate sacrifice that honoured the Intifada and condemned its opponents—a visceral and transcendent act which went beyond any reductive political framework. It was an act of humanity in inhumane times.

It is these complex events which highlight the ways a transsexual Intifada asks more of us than simple participation in pro-Intifada spaces. A transsexual Intifada is more than just 'trans liberation' in a Western, colonial sense. A transsexual Intifada necessitates that we compare our struggles to others' struggles, and reveal ways that our own understandings of a trans political agenda can contribute to less-than-radical outcomes for our marginalized comrades. Palestine continues to give us a roadmap here. For instance, if the Imagined Transpolitic asks us to believe that transgender Arabs in the Middle East can only thrive within Israel (Alqaisiya, 2020), as the so-called 'only democracy' in the region, a transsexual Intifada perspective inevitably has to look *past* the glitter and rainbows and various visual identifiers of queerness and to see the racist, Zionist underpinnings of that statement. If we are to enact Intifada, if we are to be principled in our political work with others suffering under colonialism and capitalism, we must temper our 'bottom rung' feelings[3] with the knowledge that the ideologies which seek our annihilation inevitably seek the annihilation of others, as well as trying to ensure our co-operation in finishing this task.

Schotten (2022) highlights one such connection, showing the converging co-option tactics enacted by both lesbian TERFs and Zionists. Specifically, Schotten discusses the 'extinction phobia' which both ideologies share, and the role reversal enacted by proponents of those ideologies to achieve their political goals. Lesbian TERFs perceive trans people as a threat to the existence of lesbians via (according to their theory) turning all butch lesbians into men and allowing 'men' (trans women and others in a similar category) into women's spaces. In short, trans people are diluting lesbian spaces and brainwashing butches. Similarly, Zionists perceive Palestinians and their allies (including other Jews) to be a threat to Jewish existence, as they conflate condemnation of Israel's bloody 75-year regime

[3] Justified as they might be.

with antisemitism and calls for a new Jewish Holocaust. We won't bother refuting these claims, as they are specifically formulated to be incendiary and waste as much time and ink as possible.[4] What is important to note is the effects of the convergence of these ideologies; without an intersectional, revolutionary, and humble political framework, we can see how a lesbian Jew might find herself aligned with ethnonationalist and bioessentialist ghouls, for example (Schotten, 2022).

If we allow these fear-based methods to control us, rather than alert us to an attempt at puppeteering our emotions, we inevitably fail our comrades. Any notion of a trans revolution will always remain sequestered to classrooms and clinics and cinema as long as it remains detached from the broader global struggle against fascism, colonialism, Zionism, white supremacy, and capitalism. The transsexual Intifada is our opportunity to be on the front line, to claim our place in creating a better world. This world is created through struggle, but the struggle does not have to be negative. We will finish this chapter with a discussion of how euphoria and dysphoria interplay with our affective perception of revolution, Intifada, and social upheaval.

## Revolutionary Euphoria and Tactical Dysphoria

Dysphoria and euphoria have been co-opted by the Imagined Transpolitic in much the same way many other trans issues have been. The Imagined Transpolitic positions dysphoria as an internal struggle with one's 'wrong body' (see Chap. 5), produced by only partially understood biological and sociological factors. This dysphoria resolves into euphoria through medical intervention, social transitioning, and peer acceptance. It almost seems too good to be true! All the answers seem spelled out: gender dysphoria is caused by transphobia and mysterious biological issues that seem to be resolved with some social niceties (e.g., using correct pronouns), a new wardrobe and haircut, and perhaps some (occasionally subsidized) pills and surgeries. But anyone who has undergone these personal transformations can confirm for you that indeed these are not revolutionary goals, but requests for basic human rights and empathy. If these are not the revolutionary potentials of our understanding of euphoria and dysphoria, then we need to return to notions of principled resistance and struggles.

[4] See Pearce et al. (2020) and Nejad & Babaei (2022) for more TERF and Zionist Hasbara information, respectively.

We have discussed this in previous chapters but here it is particularly important to note that euphoria in this context is *not* about personal pleasure. In particular, when we discuss euphoria with relation to the Intifada and Palestine, we have to ensure that we are upholding the dignity of the Palestinian people by refusing to sexualize their suffering as a means of reaching more audiences or making the revolution more palatable for Western readers. We cannot allow ourselves to inadvertently eroticize genocide and death, even if we believe we are using our sexuality to draw attention to the cause. Revolutionary euphoria is not orgasmic or in need of a marketing scheme. Revolutionary euphoria is about experiencing yourself engage with a higher power, whether it is people power, G-d, or both.

As we've written previously, few things are more euphoric than some direct anti-normativity action (Riggs et al., 2022). In acts of resistance, whether they are being loud on the frontline or strategizing behind the scenes, we see our personal world intermix with the relational, communal, political, architectural, and intellectual worlds around us. Not only does our perception expand, but so does our understanding of the tools we have at hand. When those tools are then used, we experience a type of euphoria that is not to do with our bodyminds, or perhaps even our spirits. Rather, it is a euphoria that is produced by connecting ourselves to a revolutionary lineage that transcends biology, geography, and chronology. We are making our future selves and communities proud, and honouring those that came before regardless of our personal connection to them (if any exists). Revolutionary euphoria erupts when we drink from the same well as millions of others, dead or living or yet to be born, who are harnessed to the task of leaving this world a better place than it was when we arrived. It is an extrabody experience; like a mind meld, our minds and souls combine to create a practical power greater than our own alone. The transsexual Intifada does not end with broken windows and disruptions to the economy and isolated comfort of the elite: that is where it begins. The rest is yet to be written.

What of dysphoria then? If we can understand that our perspective of euphoria has been minimized to exclude our personal power and responsibility, then we must apply a similar analysis to dysphoria. We offer that dysphoria viewed through a lens of Intifada and revolution is also radically transformed. The Imagined Transpolitic asserts that dysphoria is a personal grievance, an inner suffering that requires intervention, not political analysis. But what is the source of this misery? If the Imagined Transpolitic tells us we are dysphoric because of an inner misalignment, or due to ambiguously sourced negative transphobic messaging, all we can do is attempt to fix ourselves and isolate ourselves in 'safe' spaces. But a revolutionary dysphoria acknowledges that this misery holds an underlying rage,[5] and that this rage can be utilized to dismantle not only the Imagined Transpolitic but the systems of suppression which maintain it. We might also refer to this revolutionary dysphoria as *tactical dysphoria*, as it inverts the passivity and powerlessness implied in normative and clinical discussions of dysphoria, turning into a spear for us to wield.

Tactical dysphoria is many things. It is weaponizing 'ugliness', enhancing rather than downplaying those aspects of ourselves which yield visceral responses from the public. It is transforming rage into action by turning our anger towards a society that demonizes our bodyminds and lives, rather than feeling beholden to its standards. It is sitting with our discomfort in solidarity with those who can access even less than us, and finding stability beyond personal satisfaction or relief. We already live with dysphoric tension every day, it is up to us to question who deserves our ire, frustration, and most importantly political attention the most. Dysphoria often manifests in self-punishment and self-isolation, huge energetic undertaking which for many people are persistent aspects of daily life. Could we divert this anguished energy? Can we take all those words which have been used as a cudgel against us and turn them onto our oppressors? We are not repulsive, outlandish, or offensive in essence, but we can be all those things and more in order to disrupt a world that already thinks of us in those terms.

As with previous analyses throughout this book, we can also see that revolutionary euphoria and tactical dysphoria can be intrapersonal comrades within ourselves and our communities. Rather than opposing binaries, they come together into a singular transsexual political method which throws notions of both trans complacency and trans abhorrence back in our oppressors' faces. This includes those of us with trans lived experience who continue to toe liberal/centrist party lines and push for trans 'acceptance' as the highest achievable bar. Radical euphoria and tactical dysphoria show us what lies under the surface of our inner struggles, and that the solutions lie beyond hospitals, governments, and tight-leashed 'community' services. Only a principled transsexual Intifada, interconnected with

[5] More on trans rage in Chap. 12.

global Intifada struggles everywhere, could ever bring us the liberation we all deserve. Indeed, the problems we and our oppressed comrades across the world face could never be fixed in any other way. There is only one solution: Intifada! Revolution!

## References


Al Jazeera. (2024). Vatican denounces gender-affirming surgery, gender theory and surrogacy. *Al Jazeera*. https://www.aljazeera.com/news/2024/4/8/vatican-denounces-gender-affirming-surgery-gender-theory-and-surrogacy

Alqaisiya, W. (2020). Palestine and the will to theorise Decolonial queering. *Middle East Critique, 29*(1), 87–113. https://doi.org/10.1080/19436149.2020.1704505

Alqaisiya, W. (2023). Beyond the contours of Zionist sovereignty: Decolonisation in Palestine's Unity Intifada. *Political Geography, 103*, 102844. https://doi.org/10.1016/j.polgeo.2023.102844

Anderson, J. (2015). Sexual Intifada Now! Postcolonial Arab LGBTIQ activism.

Aouragh, M. (2016). Hasbara 2.0: Israel's public diplomacy in the digital age. *Middle East Critique, 25*, 271. https://doi.org/10.1080/19436149.2016.1179432

Gill-Peterson, J. (2024). *A short history of trans misogyny*. Verso Books.

Herman, E. L. (2015). Tranarchism: Transgender embodiment and destabilization of the state. *Contemporary Justice Review, 18*(1), 76–92. https://doi.org/10.1080/10282580.2015.1008946

Lindsay, J. M. (2011). George W. Bush, Barack Obama and the future of US global leadership. *International Affairs, 87*(4), 765–779. https://doi.org/10.1111/j.1468-2346.2011.01003.x

McNamara, B. (2023, October 17). Dylan Mulvaney Opens Up About Embracing Trans Joy. *Teen Vogue*. https://www.teenvogue.com/story/dylan-mulvaney-opens-up-about-embracing-trans-joy

Momen Nejad, J., & Babaei, A. (2022). Investigation of public diplomacy (Hasbara) of the Zionist regime. 143–114 ,5)2021401 نشریه علمی و تخصصی فرصت,

Pearce, R., Erikainen, S., & Vincent, B. (2020). TERF wars: An introduction. *The Sociological Review, 68*(4), 677–698. https://doi.org/10.1177/0038026120934713

Pierpont, L. (2024, March 2). Aaron Bushnell was my friend. May he never be forgotten. *The Guardian*. https://www.theguardian.com/commentisfree/2024/mar/02/aaron-bushnell-death-washington-gaza

Queer Trans War Ban. (2024). *Queer Trans War Ban*. https://queertranswarban.wordpress.com/

Riggs, D. W., Ussher, J. M., Robinson, K. H., & Rosenberg, S. (2022). *Trans reproductive and sexual health: Justice, embodiment and agency*. Taylor & Francis.

Ring, T. (2023). Elliot page embraces Trans Joy with shirtless photo. Advocate. https://www.advocate.com/people/elliot-page-shirtless-photo

Schotten, C. H. (2022). TERFism, Zionism, and right-wing annihilationism: Toward an internationalist genealogy of extinction phobia. *Transgender Studies Quarterly, 9*(3), 334–364.

Urquhart, E. (2024). Aaron or LillyAnarKitty? The complicated identity of Aaron Bushnell. *Assigned.* https://www.assignedmedia.org/breaking-news/bushnell-gaza-immolation-protest-trans-identity

Vorderer, P., Hefner, D., Reinecke, L., & Klimmt, C. (2017). *Permanently online, permanently connected.* Routledge, Taylor & Francis Group.

Wratten, M. (2023, July 13). *Mae Martin marks non-binary awareness week with proud topless selfie: "Trans joy."* PinkNews | Latest Lesbian, Gay, Bi and Trans News | LGBTQ+ News. https://www.thepinknews.com/2023/07/13/mae-martin-non-binary-awareness-week-topless-selfie-trans-joy/

CHAPTER 9

# Clinical Interventions and Euphoria-Forward Approaches

## Introduction

A key site where the figure of the trans Möbius strip is likely to come into play is in the clinical space. While certainly many trans people will live their life without feeling the need for any form of therapy, a significant number of trans people will actively seek therapy, whether that be to deal with the stressors of life (trans-specific or otherwise), or to meet requirements in particular jurisdictions in order to access medical care. As Ashley (2021) has noted, the spectre of Gender Dysphoria (capitalized here to denote the formal diagnosis) looms large in the lives of many trans people. Some clinicians may use a requirement for formal diagnosis to gatekeep access to care, while other clinicians may strategically utilize a diagnosis to support access to health insurance. And certainly, some trans people may actively seek a formal diagnosis, either through a lens of transnormativity or as a form of self-authorization in contexts where trans peoples' lives are often not taken seriously by others. But the question remains, when is a diagnosis truly warranted, and how might formal diagnosis hamper actually addressing experiences of gender dysphoria (here lower case, to denote the lived experience of dysphoria, as distinct from its formal diagnosis)?

In this chapter we explore what it means to think through the trans Möbius strip in terms of working with both gender dysphoria and gender



S. Rosenberg et al., *The Trans Möbius Strip*, Critical and Applied Approaches in Sexuality, Gender and Identity,
https://doi.org/10.1007/978-3-031-70786-5_9

euphoria, seeing them both as situated on the same loop of being, as much as seeing them as a node of the social, in which gender norms function to produce much of the experience of what it means to be a gendered being in particular contexts where gender is treated as an organizing social principle. We frame the chapter through a concept introduced by Jacobsen and Devor (2022), namely, the idea of 'prompting events'. In their consideration of both gender dysphoria and euphoria, Jacobsen and Devor speak about experiences, interactions, and observations that, for their participants, 'prompted' either dysphoria or euphoria (or both). For us, this conceptualization of 'prompts' carries considerable utility. Rather than terms such as 'antecedents'—which suggest external volition or causality—the concept of 'prompts' suggests that opportunities are somewhat more free floating, available to be taken up or discarded at will. This, to us, offers a less mechanistic or deterministic account of either dysphoria or euphoria, instead suggesting that just as the context of cisgenderism renders salient our experiences of our gender, so do the contexts we live in provide opportunities for healing, opportunities that we may actively take up.

## Prompting Events for Gender Dysphoria

Look at the literature on trans peoples' lives, and you will find endless examples of accounts of both gender dysphoria and Gender Dysphoria. Yet, in a twisted form of cisgenderism, the two are all too often collapsed. People speaking about distress related to their embodiment are often framed as having Gender Dysphoria, with no actual analysis or discussion (including with participants) about whether or not they meet a formal diagnosis. And at the same time, all too often discussions about formal diagnosis stop at the level of diagnostic criteria, paying no heed to the actual lived experience of gender dysphoria, and typically even less attention to what it means to work clinically with gender dysphoria.

Certainly, the literature does a decent job of thinking about prompting events. Prompting events may be, to a certain extent and with some utility, designated as either external or internal. External prompting events include examples such as someone misgendering a trans person, or someone commenting negatively on a trans person's body, or in broader messaging about the value of trans peoples' lives. Internal prompting events may include distress about particular aspects of one's body (such as one's primary or secondary sex characteristics, one's voice, one's hands, and so forth). Internal events may also relate to temporality: a feeling that a desired change is slow to happen, or that when it does happen, it doesn't bring about the desired effects (i.e., desired breast growth that doesn't inherently make someone feel better about their embodiment). Yet as much as we refer to these as internal events, we nonetheless must recognize that they are formed in a relationship to the social. As nodes of the social, our understanding of what constitutes proper gendered embodiment for us is shaped by broader societal norms that dictate what particular gendered bodies are meant to look like. This is not to suggest that trans bodies are docile bodies. Rather, it is to suggest that for all people how we experience our bodies is wrapped up with discourses about gendered embodiments (think here of the case we made in Chap. 3 that all care is gender affirming: expectations about gendered embodiment impact all people, not just trans peoples).

In terms of prompting events, however, less attention has been paid to how prompting events translate into dysphoria. In a sense there is a form of automaticity at play in much of the literature: an external event will happen and a person will feel dysphoric. An internal stimuli will arise and dysphoria will occur. And certainly, some of this may be true for some people. But a more nuanced understanding can help in terms of how clinicians respond to dysphoria. Context is often key. Asking about the moments, the places, the people where dysphoria is activated can help to unpack dysphoria. Too often dysphoria can seem overwhelming or omnipresent. And again, this may be the case for some people. But for many people dysphoria is context-specific.

Talking through the specific instances where external or internal prompting events lead to feelings of dysphoria can provide ways to respond. An example that Damien often uses is a trans young person he worked with, who experienced distress about their genitals. Through gentle conversations it was possible to discern that the primary context was at bath time. When they were clothed, while at times dysphoria might occur, this was less often the case. We then spoke about what it was about bathing that was upsetting. The young person shared that it was about witnessing their naked body. We discussed ways that we might mitigate that: dimmed lighting, removing mirrors from the bathroom, having bubbles in the bath. When the parents implemented these, the young person found bathing much easier. This is not to say that they no longer experienced dysphoria. Rather, it is to suggest that when we actually listen to the specificities of dysphoria, we can find 'work arounds' that can potentially make life more liveable.

In terms of external prompting events, there is often a sense in which permission giving is key to addressing gender dysphoria. Again, Damien has had many experiences where young people have shared that visiting certain relatives results in dysphoria, due to misgendering. We have engaged in conversations about the nature and meaning of the relationships, and what it means for the family to continue to insist that the young person spends time with people who intentionally or unintentionally misgenders them. Examples of things that families have tried have included writing letters to family members to explain the consequences of what they are doing, allowing young people to choose whether or not to attend family gatherings, and the entire family forgoing family events for a period of time, until other family members are able to cease misgendering. Much of the focus in terms of external prompting events relates to agency: the agency of trans people to determine our engagement with others. Particularly for young people, who may often feel or have been told that spending time with extended family is important and mandatory, recognition that they have a say in who they interact with can be vital.

As these examples would suggest, in the rush to diagnose Gender Dysphoria, clinicians may fail to actually listen to experiences of dysphoria. Similarly, while it is a starting place to listen to prompting events, needed is then a move to looking at the specificities of prompting events, and identifying work arounds. This is not to suggest that dysphoria can be entirely ameliorated by work arounds. But it is nonetheless to suggest that it is important to disaggregate dysphoria from a totalizing basket of distress with no points of differentiation, breaking it down into specificities that may be amenable to some form of intervention or work around. At the same time, we must recognize that dysphoria can be difficult to unpack, because it is so nebulous. As Chu (2018) notes, 'dysphoria is… like a flavour. Dysphoria feels like being unable to get warm, no matter how many layers you put on. It feels like hunger without appetite. It feels like getting on an airplane to fly home, only to realize mid-flight that this is it: You're going to spend the rest of your life on an airplane' (np).

## Prompting Events for Euphoria

When we come to think about euphoria, it is too easy to think about euphoria as an antidote to dysphoria. Certainly, in the literature on euphoria there has been at times a rush to position it as such, leading Malatino (2022) to argue that there is an increasing injunction on trans peoples to experience joy, often in the face of considerable hardship. Similarly, there has been something of a move towards placing an onus on cis people to help create joy for us. Again, seen as something of an antidote to the harmful effects of cisgenderism, cis people as allies are expected to do the work of creating joy for trans peoples. These types of injunctions are problematic. It is absolutely true that trans peoples are allowed to feel joy whenever and wherever we find it, however that is different to expecting that trans peoples will and must experience euphoria. Relatedly, while allyship is vital, it smacks of neoliberalism to suggest that cis people can simplistically engender joy for trans peoples, as though there is a formula for creating euphoria.

Examples of things that we see as presumed euphoria events for trans peoples are compliments and being correctly gendered. In the face of cisgenderism and harmful commentary about trans peoples' appearance, it can be all too automatic for cis people to think that complimenting a trans person assuages the harms caused by cisgenderism. Certainly, in a close relationship, or even in a clinical relationship where rapport is strongly established, saying something kind about someone's appearance may be well received. This is something many of us do with those close to us. But it can also be a trap. If a trans person talks about their dysphoria in its specifics, and a cis person says 'oh but I think you are pretty', there is a risk that dysphoria is discounted. Similarly, if a trans person speaks about more generalized distress, and someone else comments about the trans person's appearance, a) it makes appearance a salient matter, and indeed an important matter, and b) it evokes transnormative understandings of 'passing', such that to be read as cis is treated as desirable. Simply commenting on a person's appearance, then, can run afoul of the neoliberal assumption that kindness is always received in the way it is intended, and that it can never symbolize a neoliberal co-optation of what it means to show care.

In terms of being correctly gendered, the rapid rise in cis people including pronouns in their email signatures (for example), represents something of a nefarious turn in the politics of inclusion. It is absolutely the case that in its initial iterations, the sharing of pronouns was intended to take the burden off of trans peoples. When only trans peoples are asked about our pronouns, cisgenderism is at play. But what does it mean for everyone to now be expected to state or list their pronouns? First, it can be harmful to some trans peoples. Consider a trans person who has not yet disclosed to other people that they are trans. Might they feel compelled to continue to use old pronouns when asked, holding them back from disclosing or making them feel shame for not disclosing? Similarly, there is an assumption in the idea of including pronouns in one's email signature (for example): if I know your pronouns I know your gender. But pronouns and gender are not necessarily self-evident: indeed, to assume they are is to enact cisgenderism. What if my pronouns are she/her but my gender is male? If I tell you she/her and you assume I am a woman, how does that do anything to affirm my gender?

Pronouns can, of course, also be a source of euphoria. In a wonderful video, Ash Hardell and Jackson Bird talk about gender euphoria, and note that 'playing' with pronouns or clothing in a safe space can be a great way to find out what 'pings' euphoria, and from there can be a way for someone to figure out their gender. In this example, and in contrast to the one provided above, pronouns aren't presumed to determine gender. Rather, thinking through one's gender can help one to think through one's pronouns, just as exploring what pronouns work can help to provide a path to exploring one's gender. Such explorations, then, can constitute prompting events for euphoria, in that they allow for self-determination and agency, rather than a mandate from elsewhere for a person to experience their gender in a specific (often transnormative) way, and for that to create an injunction for certain pronouns to be used.

In the clinical space, it is important to a certain extent to maintain some form of separation between conversations about dysphoria and conversations about euphoria, as much as it can be important to recognize where they sit alongside one another on the trans Möbius strip. If someone speaks about dysphoria, countering this with an injunction to look for euphoria is likely to be unhelpful. Sitting with dysphoria requires just that. However, when euphoria comes up as a topic, it is also important to sit with that: to listen to what euphoria means for the person, to think through the context, the prompting events, and to talk about how it speaks to the person's gender. This is a process of reflection that isn't about the clinician 'giving euphoria', but rather listening to and reflecting the euphoria that a person speaks about.

For Damien, euphoria in the clinical space can often be in the mundane, something reflected in the words of Hardell and Bird (2018). It can be marked by major life changes (starting medication, having surgery), but it can also happen when smaller things occur, like buying clothes, or using one's name for the first time, or being hailed by strangers in a way that reflects one's gender. There is no simple list for what prompts euphoria: for each person this will be different, reflective of the diversity of experiences of gender, diversity of contexts in which people live, and their capacity at any given moment to experience joy in the face of potential challenges or marginalization. Who gets to determine what is euphoria, then, is each trans person: external attempts to create or insist upon moments of euphoria may often not be fit for purpose, though certainly those who know and love us as trans peoples are likely to know what will 'ping' our euphoria, and can help to contribute to bringing it into being.

## Concluding Thoughts

For too long, people who are not trans have sought to define us. From determining that we must be gender dysphoric and providing their diagnosis, to regulating what it means to be trans, to now often resorting to tick box approaches to making our lives better, cis people have sadly played (and often continue to play) a regulatory role in deciding what it means to be trans. With the upswell of trans people speaking about our experiences, however, this is slowly starting to change. There will always be those who seek to impose their views, whether to cause harm or from a place of goodwill. Ultimately, however, it is trans peoples who must decide what our experiences mean, even if this can at times be done in collaboration with our allies.

While gender dysphoria and euphoria might be part of the same trans Möbius strip, that is not the same as them being two sides of one coin. The latter analogy suggests that to combat dysphoria, we must simply flip the coin to euphoria. Instead, the growing body of literature and trans commentary on euphoria continues to emphasize that both function as part of the same logic: a logic founded through cisgenderism and its regulatory effects. This suggests that all people, but here clinicians in particular, must be mindful of making recourse to euphoria to combat dysphoria. Instead, clinicians may consider how both speak to one another, as much as how they may constitute quite separate experiences of being trans. Ultimately the goal should be to listen and reflect without judgement: to create alongside trans peoples spaces where the details of both dysphoria and euphoria can be unpacked.

## References

Ashley, F. (2021). The misuse of gender dysphoria: Toward greater conceptual clarity in transgender health. *Perspectives on Psychological Science, 16*(6), 1159–1164.

Chu, A. L. (2018, November 24). My new vagina won't make me happy, and it shouldn't have to. *New York Times.*

Hardell, A., & Bird, J. (2018). Gender euphoria. Retrieved from https://www.youtube.com/watch?v=9s3OlhQIZzM&t=178s

Jacobsen, K., & Devor, A. (2022). Moving from gender dysphoria to gender euphoria: Trans experiences of positive gender-related emotions. *Bulletin of Applied Transgender Studies, 1*(1–2), 119–143.

Malatino, H. (2022). *Side affects: On being trans and feeling bad.* University of Minnesota Press.

# PART IV

# Liberatory Euphorias

CHAPTER 10

# Euphoria Beyond the Binary

## On Being and Feeling Seen

The desire to feel seen by others for who you are is arguably a very common part of the human experience, one which validates our humanity. However, it is an experience which is particularly elusive for marginalized groups, who are too often denied visibility and intelligibility within Western cisheteropatriarchal, white supremacist, and settler colonial societies. Current research highlights the importance of 'feeling seen', as noted by Aboriginal and Torres Strait Islander LGBTIQ+ peoples regarding visibility on social media (Farrell, 2021), Chicago sex workers engaging with culturally safe healthcare settings (Singer et al., 2021), by an African-American man via a case study of his transformational experience within his psychotherapeutic process (Simpson, 2016), through Campbell Addy's photography project titled 'Feeling Seen' about Black Queer visibility (Huxtable, 2022), as well as by people currently receiving, or recently having received, intensive care for eating disorders (Geller et al., 2021). These accounts of 'feeling seen' are described in terms of increased visibility, validation, acknowledgement, and feeling known, understood, and accepted by others.

The studies investigating therapeutic and healthcare settings highlighted a couple of important factors in what helped participants to feel



S. Rosenberg et al., *The Trans Möbius Strip*, Critical and Applied Approaches in Sexuality, Gender and Identity,
https://doi.org/10.1007/978-3-031-70786-5_10

seen: being met with open-mindedness and receiving validation. For example, sex workers who participated in Singer et al.'s (2021) study identified healthcare providers' openness and non-judgmental attitudes as being important aspects in their experience of feeling seen and understood. Similar findings were echoed in the accounts of participants receiving, or having recently received, care for eating disorders in Geller et al.'s (2021) study. Care providers fostering trust through their non-judgmental approaches and attentive listening reportedly made participants feel safe, understood, and seen by them. Feeling seen was also achieved for some participants through validating interactions with their care providers, which felt empowering, provided them with a sense of relief, and allowed them to be themselves. The power of recognition, acknowledgement, and validation from others is further evident in the case study utilized by Simpson (2016) of an African-American man who was able to open up to his therapist throughout his psychotherapeutic process without fear of rejection. He consequently indicated feeling seen, visible, and worthy, both to himself and to his therapist.

Authors Farrell (2021) and Huxtable (2022) have also raised the importance of visibility in the experience of 'feeling seen' through social media and visual art. Farrell presents the example of Indigenous Australian trans woman Delton Clark, who believes that the key to fostering understanding is education. Clark pursues this through posting Q&A style videos on social media, which allow her to educate others about the experience of being an Indigenous trans woman. The increased understanding, acknowledgement, and visibility this affords, benefits not only her community but Clark herself, as she navigates a society that poses a threat to her day-to-day survival. Turning to the experience of a Black Queer man, Huxtable states that before creating 'Feeling Seen', Campbell Addy had described a lack of visible Black Queer photographers within the industry. To paraphrase his response to this, Addy expresses that without visibility, we can't see ourselves within society and in the areas of life which are important to us.

While there is trans representation within the research conducted by Farrell (2021) and Singer et al. (2021) on the importance of 'feeling seen', non-binary voices specifically are not present; at least not explicitly as 'non-binary' is often included under the trans umbrella and is not always differentiated from binary transness in this regard. We can, however, see the importance of exposure to non-binary identities in crafting our own journeys when looking at James' (2022) study of gender euphoria and their description of their own personal non-binary journey; in particular, their example of how impactful it was when their non-binary child associated gender euphoria with 'feeling "valid" and "seen"' (James, 2022, p. 73). While not specifically referring to trans or non-binary experiences, we also find the following quote from Addy to be illustrative of what 'feeling seen' could mean for trans peoples and non-binary peoples, particularly as we navigate the same hostile society that Clark finds herself in,

> Feeling Seen is the book I wish I could have found in that school library when I was 16. When I was that age, I wanted to see myself. I wanted to see Blackness and Queerness, but I didn't have the language to articulate it… And now I have visibility, I just want humanity. If I had seen Black photographers at 16, maybe it wouldn't have taken as long to realize I could do it too. (Huxtable, 2022, p. 71)

Feeling seen for who we are is clearly important to the human condition, especially for marginalized people who are often denied visibility and validation and are seen as being opposite to the norm when in fact we are all on the same Möbius strip of human experience—a Möbius strip that captures the spectrum of all our humanities.

## (A)Gender Euphoria

Gender is for many, but not all of us, a central aspect of our humanity and is a way in which we are seen, validated, and understood by others and by ourselves as social beings. But what does it mean to be seen as a gender, if we are viewing gender through the lens of the trans Möbius strip? And how do we find joy in our gender, or lack-there-of, when the gender we have been coercively assigned is misaligned with our experience of self? In the current state of Western cisheteropatriarchal, cisgenderist societies, these questions are taken-for-granted and treated as having answers which are so common-sense, they don't require elaboration. We are taught from birth what our place is and how we should think, feel, and behave based on the gender we were assigned at birth; through messages which range from covert in the way we are held and played with by adults around us, to overt in the way we are dressed and the toys we are encouraged or discouraged to play with. We are told who we should model ourselves after and how we can receive praise, love, and affirmation from our caretakers, as well as how to be included and valued in our social circles as they widen.

In this way, our sense of self develops around gendered pro-social traits and behaviours, which are then reinforced by our environments and relationships. We begin to feel seen by others, and then how we are seen is intertwined with a cisgenderist understanding of gender. In saying all this, we do not mean to deny the very real lived experience of gender felt by many, but not all of us, as this would be replicating the denial of one's humanity; rather, we aim to affirm that gender is, as Butler described in their book 'Gender Trouble' (1990), socially constructed and performative—serving the function within cisgenderist societies of both controlling us and determining our sense of feeling seen.

For trans and non-binary peoples specifically, the result of feeling seen as the gender we are, whether that is experienced internally or externally, can be a sense of gender euphoria, described in the current research as a feeling of alignment, acceptance, affirmation, and validation (Austin et al., 2022; Davis, 2022; Jacobsen & Devor, 2022; James, 2022; Skelton et al., 2023; Tacit, 2020). This concept of gender euphoria is often thought of specifically as being something that (usually binary) trans peoples experience, but we would argue that it isn't exclusive to trans peoples and to frame it as such reinforces cisgenderist notions that establish cis people as the 'normal' default and trans peoples as the 'abnormal' other. This is antithetical to our very understanding of gender when we view gender through the trans Möbius strip. While cis people were not excluded from the previously mentioned research on 'feeling seen', there is currently very limited research that investigates whether cis people experience gender euphoria.

One example, however, was published by authors Beischel et al. (2022) who surveyed a diverse sample of 47 people who self-identified as having awareness of the term gender euphoria. Cis women comprised 26% of participants, and cis men 2%, and although hesitant to call it 'gender euphoria', two cis participants did identify having positive gendered experiences that could be considered gender euphoria. One cis woman, for example, described the pleasure that she gets from engaging in typically 'feminine' things, like wearing makeup, long skirts and perfume, as being somewhat like gender euphoria. Beischel, Gauvin, and van Anders (2022, p. 287) proposed the use of the term 'gender pleasure' to describe both the positive gendered experiences of cis people, and the gender euphoric experiences of trans and non-binary peoples. As cis peoples' experiences of gender are seen as the default under cisgenderist paradigms, it is possible that already being seen as the gender they were assigned at birth, and thus having that part of their humanity automatically validated, their experiences of gender pleasure are less visible to the outside observer and to the cis individual themself.

If we are considering the unique forms that gender euphoria takes for trans and non-binary experiences, then the humanity this grants can be ironically dehumanizing, as it further highlights a rift between our experiences. Therefore, an argument can be made that gender pleasure alongside gender euphoria are equally important aspects of the trans Möbius strip—they are felt by all and are equally as powerful and validating, but gender pleasure for cis peoples can go largely unrecognized due to the dominance and normalization of the cisgenderist paradigm.

Beischel et al.' (2022) findings resonate with our own experiences of having conversations with our cis friends and asking them 'do you experience gender euphoria?' While their answers have varied, there has been a trend, particularly amongst cis men, of answering that they don't recognize gender euphoria/pleasure as part of their experience so much as they don't experience gender dysphoria or aren't bothered enough by the gender assigned to them at birth for it to be an issue for them. Amongst cis women, an interesting theme within their answers to this question revolved around taking ownership of and pride in what makes them feel 'feminine', such as the curves of their bodies or how they dress, similar to what Beischel et al. (2022) reported.

We are aware that the above is anecdotal evidence and to a degree we can understand how these answers arise; cis men have the privilege of not really having to think about gender in the same way as women, aka the 'second sex' as Simone De Beauvoir (2015) described it in 1949, and being an oppressed group does arguably tend to make one more aware of the characteristics that are used to define them as the other. To further our anecdotal evidence, Salem asked an agender friend (a group under the non-binary umbrella who are often forgotten and left out of these conversations) what gender euphoria means to them. They gave a similar answer to that of the aforementioned cis men; that it wasn't so much a feeling of euphoria as it was an absence of dysphoria. So, has it come full circle? From cis men not having to think about it, and therefore not strongly experiencing gender euphoria/pleasure with their assigned birth gender, to agender people thinking about it a lot, but subsequently also not strongly experiencing gender euphoria about any gender at all? Or has this been an experience of the trans Möbius strip all along? We believe that this question of what constitutes gender euphoria exposes the flaws within our current cisgenderist understanding of gender, and we say 'current' because we *have* to believe that we can move beyond these stifling notions of binary gender imposed upon us.

## Identity at Concession Price

Under the paradigm of cisgenderism and given the limited understandings of gender outside the binary prescribed therein, certain concessions are imposed on non-binary peoples who are forced to compromise in order to feel a sense of gender euphoria. These concessions that non-binary people must make in a cisgenderist society may not be as recognizable to cis people and passing binary trans people. When you start evaluating the nuances of cisgenderism and how it permeates society, however, it becomes readily apparent how much of our understanding of each other is based on ideas of the legitimacy of binary genders. As a result, anything outside of that understanding is rendered invisible and invalid. With the ever-present awareness that you are more than likely going to be misgendered in social interactions and by institutions, navigating the world as someone who doesn't fit this binary requires an exhausting amount of vigilance. To challenge this and try to feel seen as non-binary within these settings means deciding whether you want to continually expend the social-emotional energy of speaking up for yourself and educating others, when this could potentially not be heard, understood, or respected anyway. The common non-binary experience, always being aware of the likeliness of going unseen in situations outside of community, denotes the misrecognition of their sense of self and the subsequent denial of their humanity. By being filtered through a cisgenderist lens that places meanings on our bodies that do not align with non-binary lived experiences, they are not seen for who they are in most spaces and therefore denied the same opportunity for gender euphoria that binary trans peoples can experience (Robinson, 2022).

It is important to note, however, that misgendering is experienced not only by trans and non-binary peoples but cis people as well. This further demonstrates the inherent flaws of cisgenderism; someone's gender truly can't be gauged just by looking at them, hearing their voice, or through gendered stereotypes of social behaviour. Additionally, in their 2018 performance piece 'Burgerz', non-binary, multi-racial writer and performance artist Travis Alabanza (2018, p. 31) highlights the racialized aspect of misgendering, pointing out that 'to think it is only trans people that are misgendered is the whitest way to think about bodies. Black bodies have known what it means to be de-gendered, hyper-gendered, misgendered since the beginning of your slavery.' This also highlights the sinister roots of the concept of binary gender as we know it, as it was born of and violently enforced by a white supremacist and colonial agenda. The concessions placed on non-binary peoples are symptomatic of this enforced cisgenderism. The erasure of non-binary identities as a concept and a lived experience is an attempt to remove them from the trans Möbius strip altogether, just as the white supremacist, colonial agenda attempts to wipe out the authentic expressions of humanity of other marginalized groups. This harkens back to the importance of feeling seen for marginalized peoples for both validating our humanity and fighting against white supremacy, colonialism, and cisgenderism.

Granted, progress is being made in Australia as awareness is raised in the public consciousness about trans and non-binary experiences, and universities, healthcare services, and federal/state governments have implemented more inclusive language guides. However, this begs the question of what gender euphoria can even feasibly look like for those of us who don't fit cisnormative or transnormative standards of gender. Or more importantly, in a cisgenderist society in which at least part of our humanity is made up of what we socially identify as gender (a concept which varies across cultures anyway), how do non-binary peoples live their gender, or lack-there-of, in ways that can create euphoria? Does this euphoria have to be connected to gender at all, or can they forge a sense of euphoria from the ways in which they don't conform to binary standards of gender? Can they find an (un)gendered euphoria in the fact that their existence as non-binary challenges the status quo, and paves the way for a liberation from stifling gendered expectations; not only for themselves as non-binary peoples, but for binary trans and cis people as well? Through a non-binary perspective, we propose that what we refer to as gender euphoria can also arise through fucking with cisgenderist expectations, and through complicating, resisting, defying, and refusing to fit them. Non-binary peoples can utilize the power that gender euphoric experiences promote without reinforcing transnormativity, and can do so while also embracing the authenticity of non-binary embodiment. Furthermore, non-binary existence highlights the injustices and inadequacies of not only cisgenderism and binary gendered expectations, but other social processes regarding sexuality and race as well—those which Western cisheteropatriarchal, white supremacist, settler colonial societies rely on. The identification and subsequent liberation from these concessions may bring (un)gendered euphoria for not only non-binary peoples, but freedom from these Western cisheteropatriarchal limitations placed upon all peoples.

## A Personal Note on Gender Euphoria by Salem

As a non-binary person who very much does not identify with femininity or masculinity, I have seen my feelings about gender euphoria as it applies to myself shift and become more and more shaped by cisgenderism. My desire to feel seen as non-binary is perhaps not as strong as my unyielding desire to not be seen as a 'woman', and thus I have pursued gender-affirming care that perhaps in a society that wasn't based on and saturated in cisgenderism I would not have felt the need to do. Don't get me wrong, I am happy about my decisions and they have made a positive difference to how I feel about inhabiting my body, but they have not cured my feelings of what is often described as 'gender dysphoria', because my feelings of gender dysphoria are only located inside of myself in so much as they are crafted within and imposed upon me by a cisgenderist society. In the circumstances I find myself in, I often opt to be seen as a 'man', not because I in any way identify with that label but because I would rather choose the way in which I am misgendered—common non-binary concession I have to make because of cisgenderism. Consequently, the closest I come to feeling seen and experiencing gender euphoria is not in being perceived as a 'man' or transmasc, but rather in finally not being perceived as a 'woman' (or being perceived differently than I have been all my life up until receiving gender-affirming medical care). When I am perceived as a 'woman', however, I feel like I have failed; I compare myself to other trans and non-binary peoples who take testosterone and seem to effortlessly blend into the category of 'man', who you wouldn't dream of gendering as a 'woman'—like somehow it's my bodies fault it hasn't done 'enough' with the dose of testosterone it receives once every 12 weeks.

I am acutely aware that it is our cisgenderist society that is the real problem, and not me or my biology, but this understanding doesn't change how I feel in those moments; where I'm validated or invalidated because of how my external presentation is interpreted by others. Maybe the sense of gender euphoria I get arises from the choice I make to alter how I'm perceived, even if that still falls within cisgenderist standards and expectations. It provides me with temporary relief from the rejection and erasure of my gender, as was also described by trans and non-binary participants in a study on gender euphoria conducted by Davis (2022). It gives me some power over how I am seen, but I wouldn't say it makes me *feel* seen—not as the non-binary person that I am anyway.

Perhaps what *really* makes me feel seen is being recognized and celebrated as someone who deviates from the norm while knowing that what I'm actually doing is exposing the flaws in our understanding of what the 'norm' even is to begin with. That, regardless of how I'm being perceived by others or the concessions I have to make, I'm fucking with cisgenderist expectations and contributing to a future where these norms are dismantled and made meaningless as we broaden our understanding of the human experience.

## Euphoria Beyond the Binary

Anecdotal evidence aside, there is recent peer-reviewed, published evidence of non-binary people describing their experiences of gender euphoria in a way which aligns with how binary trans peoples describe it; feeling 'right' in oneself and affirmed and validated by others through their gender presentation (Austin et al., 2022; Davis, 2022; Jacobsen & Devor, 2022; James, 2022; McKinney, 2021; Tacit, 2020). Several authors, however, have also captured gender euphoric experiences and expressions that could be argued to exist outside of the prescribed gender binary (Jacobsen & Devor, 2022; James, 2022; Tacit, 2020). Jacobsen and Devor (2022, p. 128) posit that non-binary experiences of gender euphoria can be induced through the 'contradictions and instabilities' of binary gendered norms and expectations. One of their non-binary participants described how it can feel affirming for them to 'be in this strange in-between space and still feel safe with myself' (Jacobsen & Devor, 2022, p. 128). Another non-binary participant explained how, for her, gender euphoria can arise from the sense of self-determination, freedom, and authenticity she feels when she messes with binary gendered expectations and norms, by both combining them and expressing her gender outside of them.

Both the experiences of embodiment and knowledge of our humanity and who we are, and the negotiation between these facts and our environments and cultures play into our gender expression (James, 2022). The alignment of these factors is identified as gender euphoria for many trans and non-binary peoples. There is a sense of liberation in then taking ownership of our personal narratives of gender euphoria and constructing our own (a)gender journeys from them. This was demonstrated in the personal sentiment earlier about there being power in choosing how one will be misgendered, which was similarly echoed by one of James' (2022) AFAB non-binary participants. They described how choosing to dress in a way that they know will be perceived as feminine, and thus will inevitably result in misgendering, still made them feel empowered, euphoric, and like the choice was a radical one. Making a choice about how you'll be misgendered is part of the negotiation between the cisgenderist culture and environments we find ourselves in, and how we choose to interact with them as embodied peoples; it is empowering to have that choice.

It is no secret that the legitimacy of non-binary gender is questioned by others within society, institutions, and even within the trans community, where transnormative gender dysphoria tropes like the 'Wrong Body Narrative' are perpetuated. Furthermore, concerns expressed by some of James' (2022) participants that gender euphoria has become another aspect of transnormativity are not unwarranted, as gender euphoria is often associated as an outcome of receiving gender-affirming medical care and a metric of its success. However, gender euphoria is *not* a requirement for being trans or non-binary, and we should avoid idolizing it. This transnormative framing is a double-edged sword for many trans peoples but particularly for non-binary peoples, as it makes it harder for us to 'prove' the legitimacy of our gender, or lack-there-of, and be considered 'trans enough' by medical gatekeepers. To receive gender-affirming medical care under these circumstances, we are often coercively slotted into transnormative material realities and hegemonic binaries which limit our capacity for non-binary affirming alternatives; passing as cis still erases non-binary identities and leaves them illegible.

We can see non-binary peoples' lived experience reflected in the themes of (il)legibility and erasure that arise in McKinney's (2021) research. The inability to communicate their identities, a vital part of their humanity, in a way that others will understand is recognized by three of their non-binary participants as one of the major reasons for their feelings of gender-related dysphoria and distress. Regardless of whether others are intentionally erasing non-binary identities, the erasure occurs even just from the illegibility of it all. One non-binary participant described how erasure feels like 'this feeling of somebody looking at you and not seeing what you want them to see' (McKinney, 2021, p. 41). However, James (2022, p. 84) posits that gender euphoria can be 'a site for cisnormative resistance' and for practising resilience for trans and non-binary peoples facing erasure and feelings of illegibility. This point is illustrated by one non-binary participant in Tacit (2020, p. 68) study who described how gender euphoria makes them feel like they 'deserve to feel seen and be heard, and [that] not being a binary gender is okay'. Non-binary people disrupt Western cisheteropatriarchy, cisgenderism, and cisnormativity through what Bey (2022, p. 146) calls the 'gendered unruliness' of non-binary embodiment and lived experiences. This sentiment resonates with the non-binary participants mentioned throughout this chapter, who spoke of the ways in which their gendered unruliness gave them a sense of gender euphoria and made them feel empowered. The fact that gender euphoria isn't exclusive to those with binary genders and that it can arise through feeling seen for who we are beyond the binary demonstrates the utility of viewing this aspect of our humanity through the lens of the trans Möbius strip.

Furthermore, embracing an (un)gendered euphoria beyond the Western cisheteropatriarchal gender binary may allow us to dismantle the other binaries that separate us and dictate our happiness. In our beginning argument we proposed that the desire to feel seen is a common part of the human experience, and a validation of our humanity which is elusive for marginalized peoples and often accompanied by dehumanization. Trans and non-binary peoples know all too well what it means to be dehumanized by those in power, to have their humanity stripped from them; does this then make them non-human? Maybe we need to expand our concept of 'humanity' to recognize the complex experiences of all beings. If we move beyond the binary categorization of 'human versus non-human' and dismantle its underlying hierarchy, we can create a solidarity with other beings that will be foundational to forging a future in which we co-inhabit and care for the natural world, rather than dominate and exploit it.

## Resisting Conclusions

We should be careful not to put gender euphoria on a pedestal as it is not the be-all and end-all of trans and non-binary experiences. However, the improvements in quality of life, self-esteem, body image, and meaningful connections that result from experiencing gender euphoria is undeniable. While gender euphoria may not be an experience exclusive to trans and non-binary peoples, there is a certain power in using the term 'gender euphoria' to refer to trans and non-binary peoples' experiences specifically. For example, one non-binary participant in Beischel, Gauvin, and van Anders' (2022, p. 284) study described gender euphoria as 'the electric feeling of happiness and excitement in expressing one's gender, especially when that gender identity and expression are marginalized or ostracized'. This resonates with the research showing the importance of feeling seen for marginalized peoples as well. Feeling seen through (un)gendered euphoria can be an extremely important resource in counteracting the harm that can come from the concessions non-binary peoples make in order to live with the invalidation and misrecognition of their humanity in a cisgenderist society. We propose, as do Jacobsen and Devor (2022) and James (2022), that gender euphoria can be harnessed as a resilience factor that can help to combat the negative effects resulting from the concessions imposed on them by cisgenderism, as well as grounding them in the validity of their humanity, while they forge their own understandings of what gender means or doesn't mean to them. Through their very existence non-binary peoples disrupt and challenge cisnormative ways of understanding gender under cisgenderism. This challenge presents all of us with the opportunity to reframe our relationships to our bodies, centring pleasure in embodiment, and creating euphoria that moves beyond gendered views (Robinson, 2022).

Hegemonic views of binary gender demand that we repress our authentic selves, cis, trans, and non-binary alike. However, we all exist on the one trans Möbius strip and we can all stand to benefit from opening ourselves up to the full spectrum of lived experience, beyond that which has been assigned to us. This expansion can benefit not only our relationship with our authentic selves, but our relationships with other beings and the natural world as well. Non-binary peoples are a catalyst for this change as nothing disrupts the established social order quite like the existence of those who lie completely outside of the categories prescribed therein. Throughout this chapter we have asked many questions and perhaps given unsatisfactory answers, but we believe that it is important we continue to ask these questions. Non-binary people want to be and feel seen for who they are, and to feel good about that recognition—don't we all want that?

## References


Alabanza, T. (2018). *Burgerz*. Bloomsbury Publishing.

Austin, A., Papciak, R., & Lovins, L. (2022). Gender euphoria: A grounded theory exploration of experiencing gender affirmation. *Psychology & Sexuality, 13*(5), 1406–1426. https://doi.org/10.1080/19419899.2022.2049632

Beischel, W. J., Gauvin, S. E., & van Anders, S. M. (2022). "A little shiny gender breakthrough": Community understandings of gender euphoria. *International Journal of Transgender Health, 23*(3), 274–294. https://doi.org/10.1080/26895269.2021.1915223

Bey, M. (2022). *Black trans feminism* (1st ed.). Duke University Press.

Butler, J. (1990). *Gender trouble.* Routledge.

Davis, A. (2022). *Trans joy: Celebrating diverse transgender narratives.* Unpublished Honours thesis. The University of Tennessee.

de Beauvoir, S. (2015). *The second sex.* Vintage Classics.

Farrell, A. (2021). Feeling seen: Aboriginal and Torres Strait Islander LGBTIQ+ peoples, (in) visibility, and social-media assemblages. *Genealogy, 5*(2), 57–68. https://doi.org/10.3390/genealogy5020057

Geller, J., Fernandes, A., Srikameswaran, S., Pullmer, R., & Marshall, S. (2021). The power of feeling seen: Perspectives of individuals with eating disorders on receiving validation. *Journal of Eating Disorders, 9*(1), 1–9. https://doi.org/10.1186/s40337-021-00500-x

Huxtable, I. (2022). Feeling seen. *British Journal of Photography, 169*(7906), 68–81.

Jacobsen, K., & Devor, A. (2022). Moving from gender dysphoria to gender euphoria: Trans experiences of positive gender-related emotions. *Bulletin of Applied Transgender Studies, 1*(1–2), 119–143. https://doi.org/10.57814/ggfg-4j14

James, G. M. (2022). *Joy production: Gender euphoria in trans university student lives.* Doctoral dissertation. Oregon State University.

McKinney, K. W. (2021). *Imagining gender euphoria: An alternative to culturally hegemonic understandings of transgender embodiment.* Doctoral dissertation. New Mexico State University.

Robinson, B. A. (2022). Non-binary embodiment, queer knowledge production, and disrupting the cisnormative field: Notes from a trans ethnographer. *The Journal of Men's Studies, 30*(3), 425–445. https://doi.org/10.1177/10608265221108204

Simpson, M. (2016). Feeling seen: A pathway to transformation. *International Journal of Transpersonal Studies, 35*(1), 78–91. https://doi.org/10.24972/ijts.2016.35.1.78

Singer, R. B., Johnson, A. K., Crooks, N., Bruce, D., Wesp, L., Karczmar, A., Mkandawire-Valhmu, L., & Sherman, S. (2021). Feeling safe, feeling seen, feeling free: Combating stigma and creating culturally safe care for sex workers in Chicago. *PLoS One, 16*(6), e0253749. https://doi.org/10.1371/journal.pone.0253749

Skelton, S., Riggs, D. W., Pullen Sansfaçon, A., Katz-Wise, S. L., Arora, M., & Thibeault, C.-A. (2023). 'It just feels realty nice when people call me by my name': Accounts of gender euphoria among Australian trans young people and their parents. *Journal of Gender Studies, 33*(4), 470–482. https://doi.org/10.1080/09589236.2023.2285984

Tacit, S. (2020). *Joyful bodies, joyful minds: Gender euphoria among transgender adults living in Canada*. Doctoral dissertation. Memorial University of Newfoundland.

CHAPTER 11

# Euphoria and Spirit: G-d, Body Mod, the Transsexual Divine

## Introduction

Within the broader project of trans archaeology we see a movement towards trans theological archaeology; the unearthing of trans existence from the very same liturgical tracts that have been used to create our exclusion from faith and religious communities. There are traces of transness in religious texts across all major faith groups (Herzer, 2016; Sienna, 2019; Wilhelm, 2010; Zahed, 2019), and deeper analysis continues to show that gender 'diversity' can be found through many theological interpretative lenses. While this work is a critical aspect of trans liberation work, particularly in a world where trans exclusion is the dominant ideology in most religious spaces, this work tends to remain in the realm of the intellect. These types of excavatory projects are ultimately focused on validating histotheological trans existence or providing counter-narratives to fundamentalist religious standpoints—to show that trans people have been present throughout the history of human religion, and to therefore stake our claim in our communities of faith now.

However, there is a growing body of knowledge which inverts this relationship, and prompts us to find G-d and Divinity within trans (and queer) experiences (Dzmura, 2014; Hunt, 2025). Rather than proving that we 'belong' in a particular religious stream or community, this work seeks to



S. Rosenberg et al., *The Trans Möbius Strip*, Critical and Applied Approaches in Sexuality, Gender and Identity,
https://doi.org/10.1007/978-3-031-70786-5_11

find what it is about transness, genderfucking, crossdressing, and other forms of gender subversion which connects us to a transsexual(ized) Divine. Through the lens of body modification, we will explore how transness and Divinity are co-created, and consider the fruits of immersing ourselves in this nexus of experiences. We intend to use this chapter to explore how the boundarylessness of transness intermixes with conceptions of the Divine and co-creates lenses through which we might understand our role not as subjects but citizens of Divinity.

## Mobius of Divinity

Rather than dissecting individual frameworks of Divinity, we intend to speak of the Divine as that incomprehensible source to which many of us attribute creation, destiny, comfort, and/or justice. Although different frames of faith dissect their Divinity differently (a singular Divine entity, a Divine duality, a Pantheon), each has a Source from which all other Divine structures and figures emanate. Though it is known by thousands of names, we will refer to it by one of its more popular titles: G-d.[1] This is by no means an atheistic or reductive approach, but rather one which allows us to discuss Divine experiences in their broadest sense, and to consider the affective and embodied outcomes of forming a bond with Divinity regardless of the nature of that bond.

After all, G-d wears many masks (Neville, 1991), and part of the eternal game of Divinity is to try and peek beyond the masks, to reveal the true face(s) of G-d. We might think we are being presented with a multi-faceted reality, one in which the Divine has been bifurcated again and again over centuries until its original shape can never be retrieved. The spectrum of contemporary faiths and spiritual practices can make it seem as if we can only relate to G-d through imperfect or biased mechanisms, as each methodology seemingly contains irrevocable contradictions to others. How could we ever connect with G-d when the dense intricacies of each belief system appear to endlessly contradict themselves or reject other faith systems outright?

The Mobius Strip here again offers us an insight into how Divinity might be understood despite these competing systems and interpretations. In the same way that an analytic and informed perspective shows us that the supposed split we first perceive when witnessing a mobius strip is in

[1] Pronounced 'jod', naturally.

fact a single facet, we can similarly understand different faith practices as widely varying approaches that nonetheless strive towards a singular goal: Divine connection. If we understand faith practices as methodologies, as *technologies of Divine connection*, then we can also consider how other methods of existence might also carry a transcendent or Divine quality. In particular, this chapter will explore what it means to view the Divine through a transsexual[2] lens.

## The Transsexual(ized) Divine

In order to understand the *transsexual(ized) Divine*, we need to establish what a transsexual lens of the Divine entails. Fundamentally, the framework of the transsexual(ized) Divine reverses the relationship between religious superstructures and personal experiences. Rather than viewing established religious frameworks as the means of achieving Divine connections, the transsexual(ized) Divine focuses on the people who undertake these practices, and the ways their movements and embodied states produce Divine experiences across the spiritual spectrum. In particular, the transsexual(ized) Divine is focused on those experiences which are often unique to the trans experience: the modification or androgynization of one's sex; the integration of generational knowledge that is inherited through mythology rather than biology; and the metaphysical transformation of the cisheterosexual mundane through mere thought or touch.

This is an embodied theology, and it requires us to move beyond notions of 'queering liturgy' (Haldeman et al., 2023) and towards accepting our potential for uniquely trans Divine action and connection. Analysis of theological texts often positions the reader as subject to Holy words, ultimately disempowering them in the face of the towering presence of G-d and its[3] representatives. The transsexual(ized) Divine demands that rather than being subjects of G-d in its singular or myriad forms, we understand our existence as a lens through which we can witness and immerse ourselves in Divinity. By transing our sex, by finding power rather than despair in our relationship with gender, we open pathways to experiences that show us how porous our 'personhoods' can be and what active participation in the Divinity of the world could look like.

[2] Used here to delineate a trans experience that involves 'transing' one's 'sex', an embodied transformation that penetrates into our psychophysiological being in one way or another.

[3] G-d seems like an it/they kind of entity, to us at least.

Many faiths use separate aspects of G-d to construct a singular didactic Divine entity or Body. In Kabbalah and its progeny, the Divine Body consists of an interconnected network of levels of knowledge, beginning at G-d's 'feet' with Malkhut/Yesod (Kingship/Foundation) and ending with the true knowledge only revealed to Divine beings at the top (Keter/Crown) (Kaplan, 1997). Our relationship to G-d through this lens is clear: the highest order of humanity (Kings, supposedly) is the lowest realm of Divine knowledge, sitting below the foundational node of Divinity. In this hierarchy the bodymind is humbled, placed in direct opposition to ultimate Divine knowledge. The gates to this deeper knowledge are clear, but the paths through ask us to divorce ourselves from the physical realm almost immediately. Similar notions of *ascension* exist in many faith frameworks, with an ultimate goal which is aimed at moving beyond the supposed simplicity and baseness of human[4] experience and towards *ascended* or *enlightened* states of being (Jones, 1990). It's easy to see why so many trans people outright reject mainstream religious and spiritual systems. It is hard to buy into a system of belief which implies a certain necessary relinquishment of our physicality when transness inherently requires an attention to our body, and situates philosophical quandaries of gender and sex deeply within our being. It is difficult to investigate our material reality when we are told that our faith consistently calls us away from it.

The transsexual(ized) Divine eschews this bodily denouncement, and forms itself around a refusal to separate the Divine from the material, the G-dly from the bodily. Divinity is not simply a pursuit of the ultimate, most sacred ascension, whether via arrival in paradise or reincarnation or any other post-death postulation. Divinity cannot simply be positioned as a process of achieving a perfect death or the removal of our spirits from our bodies, or else our entire pre-death lives risk becoming prematurely necrotic. Transsexual(ized) Divinity asks us to consider our entire lives, and to reaffirm our spiritual connections whenever possible. We attend to Divinity daily[5]; the arrival of death is measured in seconds, but devotion to the Divine is measured in lifespans.

Through this lens, our opportunities to make contact with the Divine broaden significantly. If Divinity is a daily practice, then we are given daily opportunities to connect with this Spirit. This opportunity can be facilitated by pre-established spiritual practices (e.g., meditation,

[4] Read: physical, bodily.

[5] Even in our rejection of it.

traditional prayers), but these are not the sole entry points to Divinity. Our deepest[6] desires, our psychological and physical extremes, our fucked-with bodies, our transsexual madness (Awkward-Rich, 2022), all of these are tools of the transsexual(ized) Divine project. Some Christian thinkers have suggested that the act of transing one's sex explicitly necessitates a transformation of a person's soul or spirit (Reinsmith-Jones, 2013). Here we can see that our relationship to G-d is less dynamically skewed than many understand—if we are able to change the shape of our souls, what other Divine capacities do our actions have? As R. David Cooper (Cooper, 1997) suggests, the happenings of the Divine are in a co-reflective relationship with the happenings of the material world. In other words, we are not only affected by Divinity, but our mortal actions also echo back up into the Divine realm, changing its landscape. This means that perhaps every day, somewhere out there, an aspect of G-d has its sex changed.

We know so much now about where transness rests within the Divine. Whether it is the envaginated Christ (Gordon, 2024) or the existence of third genders in the collective Body of the Buddha (Chennery, 2016), it is easy to see how gender fluidity and complexity affect conceptions of Divinity and Divine beings. However, to gain an understanding of Divinity in transness, we need to consider the practices and attitudes of transsexual(ized) Divinity in their most material environments. The transsexual(ized) Divine is achieved through motion, through action, through relations. Therefore, we need to look at those practices and consider their relationship to the Divine realm.

## Divine Transsexual Practices

To understand transness as Divine praxis we need to radicalize our understanding of our agency in relationship with Divinity—rather than an intellectual or theological pursuit, the transsexual(ized) Divine occurs in material practices which create pathways for Divine engagement. This requires a type of *somatic inversion* (Winchester & Pagis, 2022), intentionally bringing our attention to embodied experiences which have been relegated to the background in many contemporary religious practices. This coincides with the inversion we spoke of earlier in the chapter, wherein the dominance of rigid religious structures is supplanted by the power of human action and connection.

[6] And most perverse.

The transsexual(ized) Divine does not exist in contrast to prayer, spiritual purification, or other established religious practices. Rather, it is an additional set of tools which can also been used to access Divine experiences. This toolkit can never be fully explicated, as it is subjective by nature. However, some of these transsexual(ized) ***technologies of Divine connection*** show us precisely where our connection to Divinity is facilitated. In particular, we will now explore the concept of body modification, and how a transsexual(ized) lens on the subject creates pathways for Divine practice.

## Transsexual(ized) Body Modification

There seems to be a growing and intentional distancing from the concept of body modification in many contemporary trans contexts. As we move further and further past the 'trans tipping point' (Malatino, 2016), it has become abundantly clear that we have been marching directly into the gaping maw of normalcy, homogeneity, and superficial social respectability. We have replaced 'bad' terminology such as transsexualism with more acceptable language,[7] and worked our darndest to ensure that we are seen as 'people just like you'. By extension, much of the seemingly vulgar[8] terminology previously used to describe medical interventions (e.g., sex reassignment surgery, 'the chop') have been replaced with terms such as 'gender affirming care'. This lingual shift takes away from the viscerality of gender surgery, from the intensity of radical hormonal shifts, from the ways that these interventions intentionally ***modify the body.***

A transsexual(ized) perspective calls us to return to these difficult, bodily roots. Moreover, it calls us to view these foundational trans experiences not only as 'gender affirming', but as powerful portals to Divine work. Our perception of transing one's sex has been sanitized: we have been told that our experiences are clean and tidy, that everything has been regulated through clinical protocols. In the case of major surgery, we are not even awake to experience our transformation. Despite these attempts at normalizing these procedures and processes, there is no way of meaningfully siloing the embodied experiences of gender transition away from the wider realm of intentional body modification. Some pieces of us are moved around, enhanced, or diminished as needed. Missing pieces of us

[7] Such as the increasingly meaningless 'trans and gender diverse'.

[8] Read: physical, bodily.

go away, never to return. A mound of flesh in this or that area is shifted by various means to create a new physicality. There are cuts, wounds, sickness, trembling. At the end of the day, a scalpel is a scalpel is a scalpel.

When we de-clinicize transsexual body modification, we can see transness' intimate embodied processes as something other than mere procedures. 'Gender affirming care' has a disjointed, staccato rhythm to it; weeks and months of anticipation punctuated by waiting rooms, appointments, assessments, trials and errors, recovery. Transsexual body modification, by contrast, is dominated by a more steady flow; each day, for better or worse, we touch our bodies and see where they would like to go—and then we take them as close as we can. To repurpose an earlier quote: 'Affirmation' is measured in moments; transsexual(ized) Divine body modification is measured in lifespans. When we take back our agency, even in moments where we may feel like we are at the mercy of larger systems and authority figures, we can acknowledge that their presence in our life is temporary, while ours is permanent. Similarly, when we choose to explore what lies beyond viewing transsexual body modification simply as a 'medical intervention', we open ourselves up to the full potential that lies within body autonomy, including the potential for Divinity.

By recontextualizing transsexuality within the realm of body modification, the Divine connection becomes clear. Within a Western context, the decades-old body modification scene[9] has been involved in practices that writer Maureen Mercury defined as *fleshwork* (Mercury, 2000): body modification that is ritualized, punctures and marks that are not only intended to recommit ourselves to our bodies but also to consider their porousness and malleability. This reorientation also allows us to view transsexual body modification in its broadest sense: it is not only surgeries and hormones, but piercings, tattoos, scarring, corsetry, binding, estrogenating/testosteronizing exercise regimes, and so on. Some of these experiences are physically temporary and require repetition or maintenance, while others are much more permanent. Regardless of the length of their stay, these acts and their outcomes require our daily attention. Years after a tattoo has healed, it still stands as a reminder of that initial intervention. Long after we have grown or removed body hair, we still attend to the

[9] It is important to note that this 'Western context' inevitably includes the racialized politics of the 'body mod' scene, in particular the appropriation of the spiritual practices of First Nations peoples and of other peoples from Africa and the global South into so-called 'modern primitivism' (Klesse, 2007).

sites of these arrivals or absences when we wash, when we dress in the morning, when we touch a familiar yet unfamiliar spot in our body. Each of these is a sign of our power as well as our willingness to meaningfully work with this power.

These are ecstatic experiences, in the sense that they create microscopic emotional landscapes within us that exceed the mundane, that bridge between our physical body and the broader universe. For many, experiences of intentional (and what many might term 'extreme') body modification are outright *euphoric*, even when gender is not the focal point of the experience. As we have already discussed in other chapters, euphoria continues to prove itself as an experience that is manufactured by intention as much as (if not more than) it is by the nature of an 'intervention'. In fact, if an experience was measured entirely by its perceived extremity, we would never go under the knife, mess with our biochemistry, or act on the many 'extreme' acts that are borderline mundane within trans communities. The reward or its potential, whether that be euphoria or Divine connectivity or personal exploration, clearly outweighs these 'risks' a hundredfold. This is because at the core of these extremes lies a transformative force whose effect is undeniable and whose spiritual and political mythology transcends generations.

Within this context, we can see how transsexual(ized) Divine euphoria can work as a totalizing experience, a sensation that holds diametric polarities such as pain/pleasure, destruction/renewal, or sadomasochism/healing, and creates a singular exaltational experience. Rather than euphoria representing an absence of pain or despair, it becomes a force which transcends both pleasure and its absence. This applies to those longer-term transsexual euphoric practices; whether it's taking our hormonal eucharist or sculpting our bodies in the images of David or Venus[10] through our daily regimen, we sacrifice safety and comfort for the sake of a more sacred sensation. These experiences show us that in exchange for pain, discipline, and dedication, we can receive pleasure, freedom, and loyalty. In exchange for our devotion to a Holy transsexual experience, we cultivate euphoric moments that seem impossible to conjure.

We are responsible for these alchemical transformations, these experiments in new bodily experience. Self-modification,[11] despite its relegation to the realm of the pathological (Hewitt, 1997), produces states that are

[10] Or one of Patricia Piccinini's Stags for the non-gendered folks.

[11] Whether done by yourself or with the help of others.

normally reserved for the psychedelic and/or the intensively spiritually devout. We are drawn in and out of our body, zoom towards and away from our psyches, and touch on dualities which seem oxymoronic and yet co-exist within these experiences. Transsexual(ized) body modification can make us feel invigorated fatigue, satisfying agony, microscopic G-dliness. This is transsexual(ized) Divinity—the space in which our bodyminds receive suffering and pleasure, baseness and ascension, contradictions and universal truths, as a complete package.

What does a transsexual(ized) Divine experience of body modification give its user? Rather than the promise of enlightenment, it offers us a spiritual shift in perspective. Instead of positioning us as subjects to our daily tasks, we can understand that our hands hold the power to intervene in creation, to shape our bodies away from any notion of biological destiny or (meta)physical permanence. Those parts of ourselves that we might view as stubborn, as existing in spite of our desires, those parts that we might shave or bind or tuck away each day—those parts which we might term as *dysphoric*—can be folded into a greater and more long-term understanding of how we live in our bodies and what the purpose of that life is. This is not a matter of mindfulness, but rather an intentional[12] lens we put on in moments throughout the day that allows us to remember and reimmerse ourselves in the powerful process we are already in.

To trans one's sex, to fuck with physiology or biology or aesthetic morphology, is an example of Divinity made flesh. Transsexuality exposes the horizonality (Muñoz et al., 2019) of humanity, and highlights the fact that we are yet to see all the ways in which we can exist. What is beyond our mortal field of vision but the Divine? What is transsexuality, in its most politically and spiritually radical form, if not a constant pursuit of that blurry line where the sky seems to meet the sea? This horizon is acknowledged both by those who turn towards it and those who turn away. After all, when faced with transsexuality, many people turn to G-d for answers. Regardless of whether their G-d encourages them to accept the transsexual or reject them as an abomination, the transsexual's super-natural state is acknowledged (Harlock, 2022): it asks for an expansion of what the Divine can create.

A transsexual(ized) Divine practice is therefore a practice of grappling with the ways the world asks us daily to turn away from that horizon. By denying our capacity for Divine connection, rejecting us from

[12] And for many, political.

communities, and framing our experiences as medical or spiritual ailments in need of curing, mainstream religions and broader society continues to work towards diminishing our access to Holyness and spiritual immersion. But as we have already shown, transsexuals not only have a right to the realm of the Divine, but we play a role in how the Divine is understood and connected with. It is impossible to investigate the mythos of G-d(s) without encountering gender ambiguity or downright genderfucking (Brumberg-Kraus, 2023). Through a transsexual(ized) Divine lens, we can understand this persistent textual presence from a position of empowerment. Transsexuality is not an accidental element of spiritual mythology, but an undeniable force that has been eternally bound with Divinity. Euphoria is not a commodity, a milestone, or a farfetched legend, but a tangible force we cultivate within ourselves. Divinity benefits from our existence, and perhaps could not exist without us. When we witness these paradigm shifts, inverting our role from subjects of Divinity to its rightful citizens, we can see that liturgy does not dictate our spiritual existence, it merely attempts to describe it.

## Transsexual Citizenship in Divinity

Having considered the 'position' of transsexuality and transsexual(ized) Divine practices in the broader tapestry of faith and spirituality, we would like to finish this chapter by reflecting on the material implications that this bodymind state carries. Through the lens of transsexual(ized) Divinity, we can envision Divinity as a place where we could stake our claim. Divinity is not some Heavenly realm we enter after we die, or a rare and ephemeral moment of spiritual ecstasy, but a consistent and ever-present metaphysical site for us to return to and exist within daily. Despite our increasing societal visibility,[13] we remain positioned at the outskirts of society. But this relationship too can be inverted—we do not exist at the margins, but rather we simply live *elsewhere* (Rosenberg, 2024). We are not denying the impact of social marginalization, but simultaneously we refuse to describe trans life as a perpetual process of being pushed aside and beaten down. These are real experiences, but they are not the sole descriptors of our daily lives. It is core to the task of trans liberation to consider where our power is generated, not only where it is taken away.

[13] As opposed to meaningful acceptance, which we have yet to see.

As such, the notion of transsexual citizenship in Divinity is one which highlights an aspect of trans life that remains thorny for many and entirely inaccessible to arguably many more. We are certain that reading a chapter full of unapologetic writing on Divinity would be difficult for many readers, in particular those who have suffered at the hands of fundamentalist religious institutions and other supposedly Divine entities and people. It is understandable why so many trans peoples become staunch atheists or reject spiritual discussion entirely. In our contemporary society, the majority of religious institutions, streams, groups, leaders, and community members are likely to reject our presence on a theological and ideological basis. But as we hope this chapter proves, Divinity is just another thing that has been taken away from us. Faith, G-d, Divinity, religiousness—these concepts have been poisoned, distorted, and positioned as counterpoints to liberation. But their roots, and their euphoric and transsexual potential, can always be rediscovered.

As Octavia Butler noted in an interview: ‘religion is everywhere. There are no human societies without it, whether they acknowledge it as a religion or not’ (Butler, 2005). In exploring transsexual(ized) Divinity, in separating Divine experiences from fundamentalist structures, we have sought to highlight the ‘religion’ which already exists within trans bodyminds, relationships, and ultimately societies. Our aesthetic pioneering is our ceremonial garb. Our extortionately priced surgeries are funded by communal tithes. Our perma-liminal meat sacks defy any notion of a binary humanity and hint at our Divinely unknowable nature. Our sex is Holy for it nourishes us. Our ancestral knowledge is kept alive by our devotion to our political ancestors and contemporaries. Our heroes and villains form a Pantheon that is both kaleidoscopic and ever-morphing. This ‘faith’ is already within us, and with it a euphoric potential that is waiting to emerge. All that is required is that we take on the responsibility that comes with playing an active role in the furthering of this crucial mythology, in making sure transsexual(ized) Divinity sees a future beyond our lifetimes. If we insist on an intentional spiritual existence in the face of all odds, our transsexual citizenship in Divinity is guaranteed.

## References

Awkward-Rich, C. (2022). *The terrible we: Thinking with trans maladjustment*. Duke University Press.

Brumberg-Kraus, M. Y. (2023). *The(y)ology: Mythopoetics for queer/Trans Liberation*. Punctum Books.

Butler, O. (2005). Science fiction writer Octavia Butler on race, global warming and religion. *Democracy Now*! http://www.democracynow.org/2005/11/11/science_fiction_writer_octavia_butler_on

Chennery, C. (2016). Transgenderism in Buddhism. Religious Studies Student Organization Undergraduate Research Conference. https://dc.uwm.edu/rsso/2016/panel2b/2

Cooper, D. (1997). *God is a verb*. Penguin Publishing Group.

Dzmura, N. (2014). *Balancing on the Mechitza: Transgender in Jewish community*. North Atlantic Books.

Gordon, C. (2024). *Glorious bodies: Trans theology and renaissance literature*. University of Chicago Press.

Haldeman, W. S., Budwey, S. A., McFarland, J. J., & Valle-Ruiz, L. (2023). Contemplating queer futures for liturgical studies: A conversation. *Liturgy, 38*(1), 24–32. https://doi.org/10.1080/0458063X.2022.2154514

Harlock, C. A. (2022). *Trans/super/natural: Fear, trembling, and transsexuality in American fiction*. Duke University.

Herzer, L. (2016). *Bible and the transgender experience: How scripture supports gender variance*. Pilgrim Press.

Hewitt, K. (1997). *Mutilating the body: Identity in blood and ink*. Popular Press.

Hunt, C. (2025). *Jimmy's faith: James Baldwin, Disidentification, and the queer possibilities of black religion*. Fordham University Press.

Jones, E. (1990). The origins of 'Ascension' terminology. *Churchman, 104*(2), 156–156.

Kaplan, A. (1997). *Sefer Yetzirah: The book of creation in theory and practice*. Weiser Books.

Klesse, C. (2007). Racialising the politics of transgression: Body modification in queer culture. *Social Semiotics, 17*(3), 275–292.

Malatino, H. (2016). The transgender tipping point. In *Feminist perspectives on orange is the new black: Thirteen critical essays* (p. 95). McFarland & Company, Inc., Publishers.

Mercury, M. (2000). *Pagan Fleshworks: The alchemy of body modification*. Simon and Schuster.

Muñoz, J. E., Chambers-Letson, J., Nyong, O. T., & Pellegrini, A. (2019). *Cruising utopia, 10th anniversary edition: The then and there of queer futurity*. NYU Press.

Neville, R. C. (1991). *Behind the masks of god: An essay toward comparative theology*. State University of New York Press.

Reinsmith-Jones, K. (2013). Transsexualism as a model of spiritual transformation: Implications. *Journal of GLBT Family Studies, 9*(1), 65–99. https://doi.org/10.1080/1550428X.2013.748509

Rosenberg, S. (2024). *Zipporah, queen of the desert: Living as queer and trans Jews in Australia* (1st ed.). Peter Lang.

Sienna, N. (2019). *A rainbow thread: An anthology of Queer Jewish texts from the first century to 1969*. Print-O-Craft.

Wilhelm, A. D. (2010). *Tritiya-Prakriti: People of the third sex: Understanding homosexuality, transgender identity and intersex conditions through Hinduism (Abridged Version)*. Xlibris Corporation.

Winchester, D., & Pagis, M. (2022). Sensing the sacred: Religious experience, somatic inversions, and the religious education of attention. *Sociology of Religion, 83*(1), 12–35. https://doi.org/10.1093/socrel/srab004

Zahed, L.-M. (2019). *Homosexuality, transidentity, and Islam: A study of scripture confronting the politics of gender and sexuality*. Amsterdam University Press.

CHAPTER 12

# Trans Rage for Everyone

> May you discover the enlivening power of darkness within yourself. May it nourish your rage. May your rage inform your actions, and your actions transform you as you struggle to transform your world.
>
> – Susan Stryker, *My words to Victor Frankenstein above the village of Chamounix: Performing transgender rage.*

## Anger and Rage

Out of the complex array of human emotions, anger and rage are the ones generally seen in an unfavourable light. Anger is often treated as being a problem; a negative affect masking deeper issues on the individual level and requiring behavioural modification to fix it and prevent its return. Anger and rage are sometimes used interchangeably, however while there are certainly commonalities between these affects, there are also distinct differences. Anger is the point at which our feelings are acceptable, can be rationalized, and are still potentially legible to others, but are also expected to be tempered and contained. Rage, on the other hand, is seen as unacceptable, out of control, anti-social, and destructive. Anger tells us that something feels unfair, and its cause can be identified, often in our personal and interpersonal environments. Rage arises from the sense that our wider situation is unjust and potentially threatening to our survival,



S. Rosenberg et al., *The Trans Möbius Strip*, Critical and Applied Approaches in Sexuality, Gender and Identity,
https://doi.org/10.1007/978-3-031-70786-5_12

signalling that this injustice and mistreatment is occurring not only on personal but systemic levels as well.

Both anger and rage put us in a state in which we are ready to defend ourselves against harm and both are symptomatic of our desire for change, however rage fuels a burning motivation to act against the sources of injustice and inspires transformation. Rage is a natural and justifiable response to experiencing the cumulative traumas of systemic oppression and marginalization, yet it is routinely silenced and policed by defenders of the status quo, who insist that this minority rage should be redirected into 'productive' means (read: means that leave the status quo intact, for the most part). Rage makes the reality of systemic harm impossible for good-faith audiences to hide from, and as it sews doubt in the legitimacy of Western cisheteropatriarchal authority and the forms of social control propping it up, rage is routinely punished through state-sanctioned violence and inequitable legal systems.

## Trans Rage

Cisgenderism, described by Bornstein (2006, p. 241) as a 'rigid, nearly monolithic, universal gender system', and later named by Ansara (2013), is one such form of social control. Regardless of whether we are intentionally transgressing gender normativity, we are all at the mercy of this rigged and punitive system, which relies on a bio-essentialist, dichotomous view of gender to tell us how to think, feel, act, present, and love (or not love) one another, with little regard for our authentic needs and desires. The denial of trans rights inflicts harm on individual, interpersonal, and systemic levels through the transphobic attitudes and anti-trans bigotry which are core cisgenderist tenets that inform Western cisheteropatriarchal status quos. At the heart of cisgenderism is the denial of the existence and authenticity of transness, thus disallowing trans legibility and repressing any dissent to the legitimacy of cisgenderist dogma. The cumulative effect of all this inevitably leads to a trans specific form of minority rage: trans rage. Stryker (2006), being one of the first authors to name 'transgender rage' (or what we are calling 'trans rage'), characterizes it as an affect emerging from the continual fight for the recognition of one's humanity within a cisgenderist society. Core to trans rage is a critique of cisgenderism and a rejection of the 'logics of embodiment and personhood', as Malatino (2019, p. 134) describes it, that make trans people's lives unliveable and cis people's lives stifling. Not only does trans rage act as a call to action to mobilize against systems that perpetuate and enforce cisgenderism, transphobia, and anti-trans bigotry, but it promotes trans ways of being, knowing, and becoming as well. Trans-antagonistic attacks on personhood are often what drive trans rage, giving it shape and acting as a point from which to base defiance. However, trans rage can also emerge from the frustrations we all feel at the limitations cisgenderism places on our lives, and the punitive ways in which it enforces them. Far from fuelling a separatist movement, trans rage centres itself on rejecting exclusion and creating room for all.

As a source of transformative power trans rage can be used for more than just gender-based liberatory efforts. Juang (2006, p. 708) highlights Crenshaw's intersectional framework when asserting that analysing any one form of injustice in isolation is to ignore the complex ways in which they all intertwine, and will likely lead to an 'inadequate understanding of causes, injuries, and solutions'. For example, while cisgenderism mostly goes unnoticed, when under examination its connection with Western cis-heteropatriarchy, white supremacy, capitalism, and colonialism becomes apparent. The Western notion of an immutable gender binary, which dictates one's sexuality and role in society, has been foundational to the colonization of First Nations peoples and the dispossession of their cultural beliefs, practices, and social structures (Smith, 2010). Cisgenderism too was an important tool in the construction of Whiteness, for example, through contrasting the physical differences between 'races' in conjunction with gender, in order to construct one as being more civilized/superior to the other; the chased, fair-skinned, and feminine White woman versus the hyper-sexual, dark-skinned, and masculine Black woman (Stacy aka sallydarity, 2012).

This chapter is largely influenced by and builds on Susan Stryker and Hil Malatino's work and thus focuses on trans rage; however, it is important to remember that while all forms of minority rage arise as a response to the specific conditions of oppression faced by particular marginalized groups, they are all intertwined, and can be harnessed for the benefit of all. Trans rage has a rich history of fighting all forms of oppression and calling for changes that do not strictly focus on areas of gender, but liberation for everyone. To this point, we would argue that trans rage is for everyone as part of the trans Möbius strip, and moving forward 'we' and 'us' will be used in reference to trans rage broadly, and 'they' and 'them' will refer to trans rage as it relates to trans peoples specifically.

## A Brief and Incomplete History of Trans Rage

The history of trans rage often evokes the acts of resistance to police brutality that led to the Stonewall Riots of 1969 and the Compton's Cafeteria Riots before them in 1966, and the continued fight for all forms of social justice that followed. The instigation of the Stonewall Riots is commonly attributed to BIPOC drag queens and sex workers, namely, Marsha P. Johnson and Sylvia Rivera, by those resisting the white-washed narrative that ignores them. Despite their contributions, Marsha and Sylvia found themselves unwelcome and censored by the assimilationist gay rights movements of the late 1990s and early 2000s (Malatino, 2021; Nothing, 2013). Incorporating the trans, racial, and class advocacy Marsha and Sylvia demanded risked making their campaigns seem unintelligible and unreasonable to the mainstream society the assimilationists attempted to appeal to. Marsha and Sylvia were seeking to change cisgenderism rather than to fit within its confines, an aim antithetical to that of the assimilationist gay movements, and thus it was undoubtedly a strategic move to leave them and their people behind, along with their radical politics (Nothing, 2013). Marsha and Sylvia then founded STAR—Street Transvestite (later changed to Transgender) Action Revolutionaries, who advocated for the rights of all gender and sexually diverse peoples. They called for action in addressing police harassment, the HIV/AIDS epidemic, and other social issues relating to race and class (Ellison & Hoffman, 2019). They further provided food, clothing, and a safe place at STAR House for young queens, queers, sex workers, and street kids, many of whom had been kicked out of home or were living on the streets (Ellison & Hoffman, 2019).

Marsha and Sylvia's intersecting identities are often now acknowledged in Western trans movements, however the intersectionality of their rage, inclusive of class and racial advocacy, isn't as prominent. Reducing them down to a modern interpretation of their gender ignores their complexities as people on the trans Möbius strip, and hinders our capacity to learn from their rage. They were BIPOC sex workers, who spent the majority of their lives on the streets or in unstable housing, and are now often misinterpreted primarily as trans women. However, Marsha and Sylvia never called themselves 'trans women' (although Marsha did die in 1992 before 'trans women' and 'trans/transgender' were commonly used). They described their gender using a variety of different terms: 'transvestite', 'drag queen', 'street queen', 'cross-dresser', 'half-sister' (Rivera, 2013a,

2013b). This suggests that they had a more fluid concept of gender than the labels now assigned to them allow for. When questioned about her gender, Marsha was said to retort with 'Pay it no mind'—a reference to the 'P' in her full name, and would sometimes just use the term 'gay/homosexual' to describe herself. Sylvia generally expressed a dislike towards having labels placed on her by others and described her sexuality in more fluid terms as well (Rivera, 2013c). Sylvia briefly took hormone replacement therapy but stopped when she came to the conclusion that,

> I didn't want to be a woman. I just want to be me. I want to be Sylvia Rivera. I like pretending. I like to have the role. I like to dress up and pretend, and let the world think about what I am. Is he, or isn't he? That's what I enjoy. (Duberman, 2018, pp. 37-38)

These sentiments expressed by Marsha and Sylvia likely resonate with non-binary and gender non-conforming people as they appear to reject both cisgenderist and transnormative notions of gender. In an interview with the Times, Stryker proposed that Marsha represented a style of gender non-conformity herself as she portrayed both masculinity and femininity in her presentation (Chan, 2018). These distinctions are important as they form the basis of Marsha and Sylvia's feelings about gender, which in turn informed what we'll call their trans rage; a rage with the breadth to encompass all peoples on the trans Möbius strip and their intersecting identities.

## Transfeminism and Recognition

Just like LGB focused movements, feminist movements have had their problems with assimilationism and the prioritizing of privileged members. This has resulted in a lack of inclusion and consideration for the needs of women of intersecting marginalized identities, and recognition of their contributions. Some have justified their exclusion of trans women by arguing that their experiences are different to that of cis women, however to argue this would also be to argue that BIPOC women aren't welcome either, as their experiences differ from those of white women. Focusing on the argument that 'trans women are women' also misses the mark though, as regardless of whether they are politically active or not, trans peoples simply existing is a threat to cisgenderism (Koyama, 2006, p. 704). Transness inherently destabilizes the foundations upon which cisgenderism is built, exposing its constructedness. Continuing to insist that 'trans peoples are just like everyone else' leaves cisgenderism, the system that legitimizes their oppression and fundamentally denies their existence, intact. This argument also ignores the fact that the norm through which this 'everyone' is created is based on the exclusion of trans peoples. Trans peoples shouldn't have to argue that they're deserving of rights based on their proximity to normativity—trans peoples deserve rights by virtue of their being (Juang, 2006).

Trans rage emerges as a reaction to this absence of recognition and inclusion, and the lack of addressing not only trans oppression but all intersecting forms of oppression. While rage is generally frowned upon, it is important to remember that some peoples' rage is tolerated more than others. hooks (1995, p. 15) points out the obvious racial disparities in expressions of rage, emphasizing that while white rage is acceptable, 'black rage has no place and everyone knows it'. Cowan (2014) offers the framing of the 'transfeminist kill/joy' (a play on Ahmed's 2010 'feminist kill/joy') as a critical orientation which can make room for the voices and revolutionary struggles of those left behind by mainstream liberal feminism. The transfeminist kill/joy is excluded from mainstream feminist and queer movements, finding their critical orientation and expressions of rage to have more in common with contemporary Black intersectional feminist thought, as 'trans exclusion is always part and parcel of a broader set of racialized and classed exclusions' (Malatino, 2021, pp. 831–832). This coalitional potential that transfeminism provides was demonstrated by STAR's work with the Young Lords (a revolutionary Puerto Rican youth group) and The Black Panther Party (Rivera, 2013a). Furthermore, the transfeminist agenda is shaped by a 'politic of recognition', which centres the ending of all forms of oppression, recognizing that identities intersect and cannot be separated from each other (Juang, 2006). This highlights how fluid our positions are on the trans Möbius strip, there is no fixed point when viewed through an intersectional lens. Anything else would be inadequate as no one truly has liberation until we all do.

## Purpose and Potential of Rage

When the resources necessary to our survival are continually denied, and our reliance on the systems through which we attain support are harmful to us, living in a persistent state of anger and rage becomes inevitable. Our rage may seem illegible to status quo defenders who ignore, ridicule, dismiss, censor, or punish it, however to those who are similarly marginalized, rage can signal a shared experience which validates their own and consequently raises collective care and power. Trans peoples must constantly defend the legitimacy of their very existence before their rage will be heard or taken seriously. Being dehumanized in this way can be isolating and can discourage trans peoples from organizing and voicing their rage collectively. The censoring of radical responses to minority rage has a clear purpose, as hooks (1995, p. 18) put it, 'it ensures that there will be no revolutionary effort to gather that rage and use it for constructive social change'. As is evident in the histories of Sylvia, Marsha, and STAR, the policing and silencing of trans rage can come from those within marginalized groups as well. There can be a sense of safety in 'not rocking the boat', and a somewhat misguided belief in the possibility of 'upward mobility' via a politic of respectability. When dulled down through this respectability politic, trans rage can become internalized and manifest as self-hatred, lateral violence, and self-imposed isolation from communities. Alternatively, recognizing and affirming trans rage as a collective experience can drive community building and mutual aid efforts, much like STAR did in their time. This helps challenge the narrative of trans existence as being unnatural, illegitimate, pathological, and full of suffering. Rather than expecting that we should help each other to return to a state of harmony, as is often expected of those experiencing anger and rage, the collective desire for transformation can be harnessed as a tool in dismantling the status quo for the benefit of all, not just trans peoples. In sharing these feelings collectively, we can see that there are other ways of being, knowing, living, and loving. Thus, rage is a visionary form of resistance and to turn away from such an igniting emotion is to turn away from the future and from hope (Ahmed, 2014).

When our subjectivity is one that is punished, dehumanized, reviled, and made unintelligible to others, despite it doing no harm to them nor infringing on their own subjectivity, our lives come to feel unliveable and the 'us' we understand ourselves to be feels invisible (Malatino, 2019). Therefore, the power of having our trans rage recognized by community and reflected back to us cannot be understated. In community there is the potential for solidarity, intergenerational connections, and fostering care through communal resilience building and collective healing. STAR showed the importance and power of this collective care, and demonstrated that it is possible to achieve. They were able to maintain an ongoing relationship with rage as the force stoking their connections, while redirecting its destructive aspects towards the areas in need of destruction.

Hope was undoubtedly a key part of their trans rage as well, as hope keeps political action motivated and without it, we would likely slip into despair, defeat, complacency, and even death. In conjunction with hope, trans rage holds the potential to move us beyond that which holds us back; isolation, respectability politics, and lateral violence. Instead, it brings forth the something new that transness promotes. Pulling back the curtain and revealing the farce that is cisgenderism, trans rage can eschew the normative status quo and refuse its attempts to control and assimilate us.

## Challenging Cisgenderism

Trans rage makes painfully obvious the ways in which cisgenderism controls us through pervasive normative narratives. It dictates fundamental aspects of our identity, sexuality, (a)romantic and (a)sexual desires, bodily autonomy, and the degree to which we are deserving of our dignity, rights, and access to resources. By loudly refusing to abide by cisgenderism, trans peoples push back against the boundaries of what is acceptable for everyone, cis and trans alike. Exposing the flaws in cisgenderist logic, revealing its constructedness, and calling attention to the oppressive tactics used to maintain and enforce it challenges not only anti-trans bigotry and transphobic oppression, but all forms of bigotry and oppression. The power structures driving cisgenderist dogma, pervasive mainstream narratives of natural and unchangeable social hierarchies that serve to separate us from each other and diminish our collective power, are also laid bare by trans rage which is well positioned to deconstruct them. This is the true threat to the power of Western cisheteropatriarchy, capitalism, white supremacy, and colonialism; the raising of 'critical consciousness' and the coalition of all peoples (hooks, 1995, p. 16). Our rage combined is difficult to push aside or punish, and we become harder to push aside and punish when we are united. This deconstruction then makes room for the transformational aspects of trans rage to realize their full potential, beyond just the communities it brews within, and instead carves out a new narrative inclusive of all, locating everyone on the trans Möbius strip.

In the spirit of this, it may be more appropriate to consider the 'trans' in trans rage to not only mean 'transgender', but a more intersectional and all-encompassing *transformational* as well. Adding 'transformational' was first suggested by Cowan (2014) who wished to expand on Stryker, Currah, and Moore's (2008, p. 11) original proposal of 'trans-' as meaning 'Trans: -gender, -national, -racial, -generational, -genic, -species'. She elaborated on this addition by saying that 'the crossing implied by transformational is the crossing between structures, between systems, between selves', thus further expanding the meaning of trans rage as well (Cowan, 2014, p. 506). The consideration of '-species' in the expansion of 'trans-' also holds the potential to challenge the speciesism and human exceptionalism that props up hierarchies of power, like cisgenderism, and legitimizes systems of domination over the natural world (Skelton & Riggs, 2024). Trans peoples occupy a liminal space in Western cisheteropatriarchal constructions of 'nature'. Cisgenderist logics routinely dehumanize trans peoples while simultaneously denying their existence as a part of nature, instead accusing them of espousing beliefs about gender and sex that go against the supposedly established truths of 'basic biology'. Trans rage can help us to think through not only what it means to exist as beings outside of Western cisheteropatriarchal hierarchies, but what it means to exist outside the binaries of 'human/non-human', and 'natural/unnatural' as well. The transformational potential of this expanded perspective may drive the radical restructuring that is required to build a co-habitable future for all life on our planet, as it faces the existential threat of ecological collapse.

Furthermore, when contemplating the use of the term 'transphobia' as indicating fear and hatred of trans peoples, Bornstein (2006) posits that it would be a more effective descriptor if it had the breadth to extend its meaning to hatred and fear of those who *transgress* any kind of perceived societal border. Gender transgression is a political act whether the transgressor intends it to be or not, which deconstructs not only gender but all Western cisheteropatriarchal hierarchies and social strata. It may also be appropriate then to include 'transgressors' in the meaning of 'trans' in trans rage, as attacks on trans peoples are indicative of a cisgenderist system that readily attacks cis people who transgress cisgenderist norms and expectations as well. Going back to the original proposal of an expansion in its meaning, Stryker et al. (2008, p. 14) suggest 'trans-' as being representative of the body and the ways in which it connects and flows through the 'macros- and micro- political registers'. All bodies become entangled in the formations of what we call 'nations', 'states', and the capital they claim through the extraction of natural resources, and the exploitation of human and non-human beings (Stryker et al., 2008). '-gender' is but one of the variable techniques through which bodies are made to matter, and our lives are assigned meaning and purpose in service of Western cisheteropatriarchal, white supremacist, capitalist, and settler colonial agendas. Rather than being associated with a state of 'crossing' or 'in between', this expansion of 'trans' then *becomes* the trans Möbius strip and trans rage becomes the language of liberation for all it encompasses.

## Conclusion

Minority rage manifests itself as a response to the cumulative traumas of living under conditions which are unsupportive of our needs and desires, actively works against us, and is hostile to our existence. Trans rage arises from the cisgenderist aspects of these conditions which are not only hostile to trans existence, but deny its legitimacy out right in favour of a bio-essentialist view of gender. The socio-political and cultural legibility afforded to those with privilege means that their expression of rage is justified and righteous, whereas the rage of minorities is not and is instead censored, dismissed, ignored, and punished. This has been a common experience for activists like Sylvia Rivera, Marsha P. Johnson, and the group STAR, whose trans rage was unwelcome by assimilationist LGB focused and liberal feminist movements. Transness and trans rights advocacy are destabilizing not only to cisgenderism but to Western cisheteropatriarchy, white supremacy, capitalism, and colonialism as well. Expressing trans rage was, and continues to be, seen as detrimental to the assimilationist agenda and is consequently deprioritized, and sometimes out-right rejected. Conversely, transfeminist orientations recognize intersectionality and incorporate the struggles of all minority groups. Treating both rage and love as part of a coalitional politic encourages reparations, transformative resistance, and the possibility of change for all.

We fight somewhat of an uphill battle in harnessing the power of trans rage, and have for a long time. Revolting against oppressive systems is no easy feat, and we still need to exist within these systems to survive in the meantime. This is why we need everyone on board, deconstructing their internalized cisgenderism, and exploring their identities for themselves. By weaponizing the transformational power of trans rage, we can dismantle cisgenderism and liberate all beings from the stifling limitations on our self-determination, and the punishment of transgression from prescribed norms, for cis and trans alike. Trans rage can bring people together to build community, foster solidarity, provide mutual aid, and collectivize our rage as a revolutionary act of joy and hope. Through a coalitional transfeminist politic of recognition which rejects an 'us-vs-them' mentality, and instead recognizes that all people are part of the trans Möbius strip, we can see that there is no need to locate an 'other'; we're all being duped by the same flawed logic of the cisgenderist systems dictating our lives. Thus the 'trans' in trans rage necessarily encompasses everyone, as we all *trans*gress cisgenderist norms at some point, whether we intend to or not, and we would all benefit from a *trans*formation of our ways of living, knowing, loving, and being outside of the confines of cisgenderism. And *this* is why trans rage is for everyone.

## References

Ahmed, S. (2014). *The cultural politics of emotion* (2nd ed.). Edinburgh University Press.

Ansara, Y. G. (2013). *Cisgenderism: A bricolage approach to studying the ideology that Delegitimises People's own designations of their genders and bodies* (Publication Number: 27558163) [Doctoral dissertation, University of Surrey]. ProQuest.

Bornstein, K. (2006). Gender terror, gender rage. In S. Stryker & S. Whittle (Eds.), *The transgender studies reader* (pp. 236–243). Routledge.

Chan, S. (2018, March 8). Marsha P. Johnson: A transgender pioneer and activist who was a fixture of Greenwich Village street life. *The New York Times*. https://www.nytimes.com/interactive/2018/obituaries/overlooked-marsha-p-johnson.html

Cowan, T. L. (2014). Transfeminist kill/joys: Rage, love, and reparative performance. *Transgender Studies Quarterly, 1*(4), 501–516. https://doi.org/10.1215/23289252-2815201

Duberman, M. (2018). *Has the gay movement failed?* University of California Press.

Ellison, J., & Hoffman, N. (2019). The afterward: Sylvia Rivera and Marsha P. Johnson in the medieval imaginary. *Medieval Feminist Forum: A Journal of Gender and Sexuality, 55*(1), 267–294.

hooks, b. (1995). *Killing rage: Ending racism*. Henry Holt & Company.

Juang, R. M. (2006). Transgendering the politics of recognition. In S. Stryker & S. Whittle (Eds.), *The transgender studies reader* (pp. 706–719). Routledge.

Koyama, E. (2006). Whose feminism is it anyway? In S. Stryker & S. Whittle (Eds.), *The transgender studies reader* (pp. 698–705). Routledge.

Malatino, H. (2019). Tough breaks: Trans rage and the cultivation of resilience. *Hypatia, 34*(1), 121–140. https://doi.org/10.1111/hypa.12446

Malatino, H. (2021). The promise of repair: Trans rage and the limits of feminist coalition. *Signs: Journal of Women in Culture and Society, 46*(4), 827–851. https://doi.org/10.1086/713292

Nothing, E. (2013). Queens against society. In E. Nothing (Ed.), *Street transvestite action revolutionaries: Survival, revolt, and queer antagonist struggle* (pp. 3–11). Untorelli Press.

Rivera, S. (2013a). "I'm glad I was in the stonewall riot": An interview with Sylvia Rivera. In E. Nothing (Ed.), *Street transvestite action revolutionaries: Survival, revolt, and queer antagonist struggle* (pp. 12–14). Untorelli Press.

Rivera, S. (2013b). Transvestites: Your half-sisters and half-brothers of the revolution. In E. Nothing (Ed.), *Street transvestite action revolutionaries: Survival, revolt, and queer antagonist struggle* (pp. 19–20). Untorelli Press.

Rivera, S. (2013c). Queens in exile, the forgotten ones. In E. Nothing (Ed.), *Street transvestite action revolutionaries: Survival, revolt, and queer antagonist struggle* (pp. 40–55). Untorelli Press.

Skelton, S., & Riggs, D. W. (2024). Exploring the more-than-human in trans people's lives: Connections, sociality, being and animal companionship. *International Journal of Transgender Health*, 1–10.

Smith, A. (2010, July/August). Dismantling hierarchy, queering society. Tikkun, *25*, 4. https://www.tikkun.org/nextgen/2010/07/01/dismantling-hierarchy-queering-society/

Stacy aka sallydarity. (2012). Gender sabotage. In C. B. Daring, J. Rogue, D. Shannon, & A. Volcano (Eds.), *Queering anarchism: Addressing and undressing power and desire* (1st ed., pp. 43–62). AK Press.

Stryker, S. (2006). My words to victor Frankenstein above the village of Chamounix: Performing transgender rage. In S. Stryker & S. Whittle (Eds.), *The transgender studies reader* (pp. 244–256). Routledge.

Stryker, S., Currah, P., & Moore, L. J. (2008). Introduction: Trans-, trans, or transgender? *Women's Studies Quarterly, 36*, 11–22.

# Postface

As we end this book, as much as we hope it but one entry point in ongoing conversations about how we live our lives as trans people, it is useful to revisit some of the ground covered. Throughout this book we have, in differing ways, worked with the figure of the trans Möbius strip. In places this has involved something of a deeper dive into how we think about social structures, social norms, and individual actions. In other places we have used it lightly, as a motif for thinking beyond binaries, or indeed highlighting and challenging binaries. As we suggested in the preface of this book, the figure of the trans Möbius strip is not intended to serve as yet another operationalized, definitive, restrictive way of thinking about trans lives. Instead, it is akin to a leitmotif: something that might motivate us to speak to one another, to resist restrictions, and to continue to explore ways of thinking about our lives.

If anything, the figure of the trans Möbius strip calls into question who counts as trans. Is trans bounded by transnormative rules about medical treatment and social transition? Or is trans also a mode of being, a mode of relationships, and a way of seeing the world (Stryker et al., 2008)? Our answer would be that the trans Möbius strip is all of that and more. Without wishing to be obtuse, we would suggest it can be anything that you, as our reader, wish it to be. Our starting point for writing this book was conversations between Shoshana and Damien about the limiting ways



S. Rosenberg et al., *The Trans Möbius Strip*, Critical and Applied Approaches in Sexuality, Gender and Identity,
https://doi.org/10.1007/978-3-031-70786-5

in which dysphoria is thought about, alongside conversations between Salem and Damien about how we define, witness, and identify gender euphoria. This book is a product of those early conversations, while itself having taken on a whole new life. While we first intended the book to be much more definitive, the end product has been yet another series of conversations between us as authors and within us as individuals. It has been a process of unpacking the taken for granted, while at the same time often writing things that we take for granted, but which we are guessing might be new for some readers.

As such, we hope that as a reader you have received this book in the spirit it is intended: to prompt conversation, to continue existing dialogues, and to contribute to new lines of thinking. Too often, our lives as trans peoples are framed as singular, in isolation, while at the same time we are too often framed by conservatives as a collective menace to be quashed. Through this book, we have claimed that we are indeed diverse peoples, a collective brought together by the harmful effects of cisgenderism but differentiated by our experiences, our locations, and the individual realms of (in)telligibility that we occupy. Just as there is no singular experience of dysphoria or euphoria, there is no singular experience of being trans. The figure of the trans Möbius strip, we hope, provides you with a way of thinking about the singular through the universal, situating ourselves in relationships that are part of a long and rich history of trans existence.

## Reference

Stryker, S., Currah, P., & Moore, L. J. (2008). Introduction: Trans-, trans, or transgender? *Women's Studies Quarterly, 36*, 11–22.

# Index[1]


**A**
Affective, 6, 16, 58–60, 86, 116
Affirming care, 15, 16, 20, 23–29, 33–40
Agnes, 27
Anger, 88, 129–130, 134, 135
Animals, 24, 75

**B**
Bodymind, 42–45, 47, 56, 57, 62, 87, 88, 118, 123–125
Body modification, 39, 116, 120–124

**C**
Capitalism, 55, 85, 86, 131, 136, 138
Children, 17, 25, 26
Cisgenderism, 5, 9–11, 13, 17, 26, 27, 33, 71, 75–77, 92, 95–97, 106–108, 111, 112, 130–134, 136–139, 142
Colonialism, 83, 85, 86, 107, 131, 136, 138
Concession, 106–109, 112
Crip, 41–53

**D**
Divinity, 115–121, 123–125

**E**
Embodiment, 11, 16, 17, 19, 29, 34–36, 40, 44, 65n14, 92, 93, 107, 109, 111, 112, 130
Enarees, 27
Eugenics, 24, 44

**F**
Family, 35, 37, 49, 59, 71–77, 94
Fractures, 71–77


[1] Note: Page numbers followed by 'n' refer to notes.






S. Rosenberg et al., *The Trans Möbius Strip*, Critical and Applied Approaches in Sexuality, Gender and Identity,
https://doi.org/10.1007/978-3-031-70786-5

Freedom, 46, 49, 62, 84, 108, 109, 122
Fucking, 55–66, 107, 109

**G**
Gender dysphoria, v, 4, 9–11, 13–20, 63, 86, 91–94, 97, 105, 108, 110
Gender euphoria, v, 4, 11, 13, 14, 17–20, 24, 91–92, 96, 102–112, 142
Growth, 48, 73–77, 93

**H**
Healing, 19, 71–77, 92, 122, 135
History, 4, 14, 17, 24, 27, 44, 45, 61, 65, 115, 131–133, 135, 142
Honour-based, 71

**K**
Kinship, 49–53, 75

**L**
Loss, 34–36, 40, 72, 73, 75

**M**
Mayhem laws, 15, 26
Medical, 14–16, 18, 20, 24–29, 35–40, 43, 48, 55, 81, 83, 84, 86, 91, 108, 110, 120, 121, 124, 141
Modality, 8–9, 24, 66

**N**
Non-binary, 8, 19, 65, 102–112, 133

**P**
Palestine, 45, 46, 83–85, 87
Primarine, 27
Prompting events, 92–97

**Q**
Queer Black visibility, 101

**R**
Rage, 51, 52, 88, 129–139
Resistance, v, 9, 20, 26–28, 42, 46, 47, 50–52, 86, 87, 110, 132, 135, 138
Revolution, 45–47, 51, 52, 61–63, 83, 86, 87

**S**
Surgery, 25–28, 34, 35, 39, 40, 97, 120

**T**
Transition, 18–20, 36, 37, 39, 51, 61–63, 73, 120, 141
Trans Möbius strip, v, vi, 3–11, 13, 14, 17, 20, 24, 29, 33–35, 46, 71, 77, 91, 96, 97, 103–105, 107, 111, 112, 131–134, 136, 138, 139, 141, 142

Transnormativity, 16, 36, 79–81, 91, 107, 110
Transpolitics, 79–89
Transsexual divine, 115–125
Transsexual Intifada, 79–89
Trauma, 33–40, 74, 130, 138

V
Violence, 33, 41, 42, 44, 45, 66, 130, 135, 136

W
Wrong body, 16, 41–53, 86

SPRINGER NATURE

# GPSR Compliance

*The European Union's (EU) General Product Safety Regulation (GPSR) is a set of rules that requires consumer products to be safe and our obligations to ensure this.*

*If you have any concerns about our products, you can contact us on ProductSafety@springernature.com*

In case Publisher is established outside the EU, the EU authorized representative is:

Springer Nature Customer Service Center GmbH
Europaplatz 3
69115 Heidelberg, Germany

The manufacturer's authorised representative in the EU is Springer Nature Customer Service Centre GmbH, Europaplatz 3, 69115 Heidelberg, Germany. If you have any concerns regarding our products, please contact ProductSafety@springernature.com

Printed and bound by CPI Group (UK) Ltd, Croydon, CR0 4YY
01/10/2026
02225879-0007